Contents

Preface: English, Language and Literacy 3 to 19   3
- Purpose   3
- Key principles   4
- The booklets   5
- The National Curriculum   5

1. Media – summary of main points   6

2. Media education: four patterns   7
- The first pattern: media education as suspicious reading   7
- The second pattern: media education's fact/fiction divide   7
- The third pattern: media education as reading not writing   8
- The fourth pattern: media texts as poor relations of literature   8

3. Media education in the UK: a brief history   10
- Phase one   10
- Phase two   10
- Phase three   10
- A history of defensiveness   10
- Connections with the sociology of childhood and with literacy   11
- The British Film Institute   11
- Key questions   11
- Media literacy   12
- Associations of media educators   12
- Current structures and practices   13

4. A model for media education   14
- Let the cousins continue to kiss   14
- Cultural distinction   14
- Rhetoric and poetics   18
- Creative production   21

5. More examples of media education in practice   24
- Animation in the primary school   24
- Comic-strip superheroes   25
- TV hospital dramas   26
- Designing games   30
- Teaching *Psycho*   33
- Selling chocolate   34
- Filming performed poetry   36

continues over

6. An outline framework for a media-education curriculum   38

- Introduction   38
- The framework's structure   39
- Early Years Foundation Stage   39
- Key Stage 1   39
- Key Stage 2   40
- Key Stages 3 and 4   41

7. Conclusion: beyond the old divides   42

References   43

Acknowledgements

This booklet draws on a variety of research projects and teachers' practice. I am grateful in particular to former colleagues David Buckingham, Becky Parry and Mandy Powell, whose work on the Developing Media Literacy project (Economic and Social Research Council 2009-2012) I draw on here. I also owe a considerable debt to James Durran, Craig Morrison and Anthony Partington, whose inspiring classroom work is represented at various points in the booklet. I thank my colleagues in the DARE research group, John Potter, Mark Reid and Theo Bryer, whose insights into media education continue to fuel fresh thoughts. I am grateful to Bronwyn Mellor for her careful proofreading of the final text.

Andrew Burn

Preface: English, Language and Literacy 3 to 19

Purpose

This booklet is one of a series about the teaching of language, literacy and English to children and young people aged 3 to 19. The aim of the series is to inspire and inform debate about school strategy. The booklets draw on seminal studies and development work carried out over many years. They have been commissioned by Owen Education, an independent school-improvement agency.

Owen Education's purpose in producing the series is easily stated. There should, in the second decade of the 21st century, be a professional consensus amongst those who teach English to children and young people, or who teach those children and young people *in* English, as to how to help them most effectively gain confidence and competence in the use of English. We observe that though this consensus *should* exist, in practice it does not. We aim here to describe a desirable, intellectually sound and practically achievable consensus around which those who teach English or teach *in* English could unite.

By 'those who teach English or teach *in* English' we mean three groups of professionals: teachers of children aged from three to 11 in early-years settings and primary schools; teachers of the subject English in secondary schools and colleges serving young people between the ages of 11 and 19; and teachers of a range of other subjects in those secondary schools and colleges, for whom it is essential that students have sufficient confidence and competence as readers, writers and speakers of English to access and benefit from the curriculum in those subjects.

There is a particular urgency in our purpose, since all contemporary commentators agree that, whatever progress has been made overall in raising the achievement of learners in English, language and literacy, there is still a large gap between the highest and the lowest achievers. There are still far too many children and young people who are failing to become competent and confident users of English, when there is no valid reason, in terms of their potential, why they *should* fail. Those most at risk of failure are learners from socio-economically poorer backgrounds.

Key principles

We believe that the best work on the development of language and literacy draws on seven basic principles.

1. There is no intellectual achievement more intimately connected to a child's and young person's overall sense of worth as an individual and as a social being than the achievement of competence and confidence in the use of her or his language or languages.

2. The achievement of competence in any aspect of language is prior to and more complex than the achievement of the ability to analyse that aspect of language. Learners nonetheless continually engage in acts of reflection on aspects of the language they encounter and use.

3. The achievement of competence in any aspect of language is principally owed to the enjoyable *experience* of that aspect of language. *Instruction* in an aspect of language has a secondary but nonetheless very significant role to play in this achievement.

4. The learner's brain makes dynamic generalisations from enjoyable experiences of language. These generalisations prepare the learner for new encounters with and uses of language.

5. The motivation for any productive or receptive encounter with or use of language is the desire and need to construct meaning. Producers and receivers of language are both engaged in the construction of meaning.

6. Examples of language and literacy in use in English and of potential value and interest to learners are vast in number and diversity. Some of that diversity should be evident in the selection of examples which teachers present to learners.

7. Learners' experience of language in education should both value and confirm their linguistic, cultural and social backgrounds, and introduce them to cultural and social contexts beyond those they are familiar with.

The seven principles are stated here at a level of generality and abstraction which probably seems high-flown and dry. We shall try to invest them with a living practicality later on. In the meantime, it may be asked: what is so remarkable about them? Are they not self-evident, uncontroversial? The answer is: they should be, but they haven't been. The reason why they haven't been has something to do with the history of the contest for control of the teaching of English, language and literacy in our schools and colleges over the last five decades. It also has to do with the fact that worthwhile professional knowledge can sometimes be forgotten, get lost, in the welter of new initiatives and changes of direction – often politically driven – affecting the curriculum.

The booklets

The series sets out and illustrates a comprehensive and rigorous basis on which learners are enabled to gain confidence and competence in the use of English. The booklets are entitled:

English, Language and Literacy 3 to 19: Summary
Talk
Reading 3 to 7
Writing 3 to 7
Reading 7 to 16
Writing 7 to 16
Grammar and Knowledge about Language
Drama
Media
English 16 to 19

The National Curriculum

We believe that the new National Curriculum for English, taking effect from September 2014 or September 2015, contains so many ill-judged requirements, so much legally binding content which runs contrary to the way in which children and young people most effectively learn English (whether as their first or additional language), that we have been driven to offer an alternative. This is set out in its entirety in the summary booklet for the whole series, and in chapters in the booklets dealing with any part of the 5 to 16 curriculum.

At some point in the future, government and the profession will have to sit down together and make something better than has been made now, because significant sections of the new orders will prove to be unworkable.

We welcomed the original principle of the National Curriculum, introduced in 1989 and 1990, which was to offer a broad statement of the knowledge, skills and understanding to which all students in state schools in England and Wales were and are entitled. We lament the absurdity of the current situation, whereby a majority of state secondary schools and a growing minority of primary schools – those that are academies and free schools – are not bound by the National Curriculum. Why go to all the trouble of designing a legally enforced National Curriculum and then abandon the principle of general entitlement? This is an incoherent and inequitable position.

John Richmond
Peter Dougill
Mike Raleigh

1 Media – summary of main points

In the past, media education has often been seen as a form of 'inoculation': of protection against the cultural, moral and ideological ill effects of the mass media. More recently, media education has struck a more positive note. Its emphasis is on the value of popular culture, and on the importance of media forms such as cinema, television, comic books, video games, animation, advertising, news media and social media in representing our world.

Media education in the National Curriculum in England has been contained within English. This has provided positive opportunities for teachers and learners, raising the profile of moving-image texts, introducing the idea of multimodal texts, and emphasising the importance of digital media. However, media education's place within English has also caused problems: emphasising factual media at the expense of fiction; suggesting a 'suspicious' mode of reading media texts (in contrast to the 'appreciative' mode expected for literary texts); and restricting media education to the reading section of the curriculum, thus making it mandatory to 'read' media texts, but not to 'write' them.

In the most recent version of the National Curriculum for English, media education has effectively been expunged. It should be fully reinstated. Any adequate media curriculum should equally emphasise 'reading' (analysis of media) and 'writing' (production of media).

Media education can be a separate subject in the curriculum. That is how it is most strongly represented in the UK in post-14 education, in the form of specialist Media Studies and Film Studies syllabuses. While the popularity of these post-14 courses is welcome, media education 3 to 16 is best located within English. This arrangement allows for a coherent approach to the study and making of texts and meanings across all media, which can extend and strengthen students' understanding of textual structures, contexts and functions. It is the arrangement most likely to provide entitlement to media education for all young people in the school system.

The study of media, drama and literature together within English allows teachers and students to explore the spectrum of cultural taste, from elite canonical texts through to popular cultural forms, and the increasing tendency for these to collapse into one another. The contrasting modes of engagement with texts characteristic of media and literary studies in schools, 'rhetorical' and 'poetic' stances respectively, are stronger if united.

A media education curriculum from 3 to 16, involving 'reading' the media, 'writing' the media, and engaging with the contexts in which media practices occur, must be recursive. It cannot artificially distribute certain kinds of work across 'ages and stages', but should suggest how the same work (for example, editing a film) might change, expand, become more challenging and diverse, as students get older, gain more experience and become more autonomous.

2 Media education: four patterns

A glance at the construction of media education in the English curriculum reveals four patterns which make useful starting points for a consideration of what is happening in media education now, and what might develop in the future.

The first pattern: media education as suspicious reading

These four patterns follow a common theme, set by the first pattern, in which media education has been constructed as a kind of suspicious reading, pushing teachers and students towards the scrutiny of newspapers and television programmes to detect bias, misrepresentation and other distortions of some imagined truth.

Behind this suspicious reading lies a tangled history of protectionist impulses, clearly identified by David Buckingham in his *Media Education: Literacy, learning and contemporary culture* (2003), and further explored below: impulses to protect children from what are seen as the various debilitating effects of the mass media, whether such effects be cultural, ideological or moral. While these impulses may be considerably stronger in the US than in the UK (or indeed in European media education in general), they are nevertheless a factor in the institutional regulation of media texts for young people, and in the value systems sometimes applied to schools' choice of texts.

The second pattern: media education's fact/fiction divide

The second pattern discernible in curricular constructions of media in English is that media have often been imagined as a genre of factual representation and communication: essentially, news media. It's as if the entire function of narrative texts and imaginative fiction is reserved for literature. Two histories are noteworthy here. One features F. R. Leavis, whose critical readings of media texts for school students never embraced the narrative structures of comic strips or the poetics of film, but rather made advertising their object of attack (Leavis and Thompson, 1933/1977). Leavis notoriously invented many of the advertising texts he used, the better to exemplify their debased nature.

The other history in this second pattern helps to explain how, regrettably, media literacy is now once again only being seen as a matter of how citizens retrieve and critically appraise factual information. This is the history of the computer. As Lev Manovich has memorably described, the computer, from its inception in the form of Babbage's Analytical Engine in the 1830s, has developed as a processor of information, in contrast to the history of photography (also beginning in the 1830s with Daguerre's daguerreotype), which is a history of cultural representations (Manovich, 1998).

As these two technologies have become fused in the multimedia computer, ICT educators are having difficulty understanding how the number-cruncher has become a tool of cultural production; while media and English teachers struggle with the implications of the cultural representations which have been their traditional stock-in-trade – films, poems, stories – becoming computable. It is partly for this reason that computer games, a cultural form which has always by definition been a set of computable representations, pose such interesting and challenging questions for media and English teachers as they consider how to teach such a form in the classroom (a question to which chapter 3 will return).

In the wider world of policy, some politicians and officials have continued to be trapped by this division of media into, effectively, fictions on the one hand and factual information on the other. In Europe at least, the fictions have been largely the interest of film educators, who have considered how cinema narratives can be critically explored in schools in much the same appreciative way that literature teachers deploy in their approach to literary fictions. Meanwhile, the policy-makers have been largely preoccupied with how factual information is conveyed to citizens through electronic media, particularly online.

So, the general effect of this fact/fiction divide in the educational and policy arenas is to overemphasise both the importance and the risks of factual information in young people's lives, and to almost completely neglect the most important uses young people actually make of the media: the music, dreams, fantasies, play, dramatic narratives, whimsical performances, album-making, aspirational self-representation, parodic invention and casual communication which make up most of their online lives.

The third pattern: media education as reading not writing

The third pattern in the construction of media in the English curriculum is that it represents, essentially, an act of critical reading. Media within English has been located within the reading section of the curriculum, with no equivalent provision made in the writing section. In England, it has been mandatory since the inception of the National Curriculum for English to teach children to *read* the media (that is, critically interrogate it), but not to *write* it (that is, produce their own media texts) (Qualifications and Curriculum Authority, 2007). (But see the last section of the next chapter for an account of the abandonment of even this requirement in the new National Curriculum for English.) There is a doubly suspicious stance here: a suspicion, again, of media texts, positioning them as objects of a critical gaze quite different from that envisaged for literature; but also a suspicion of young people's own media production work, implicitly devalued by comparison with creative writing.

There have been, indeed, criticisms of student media productions within the media education community, castigating some of them as incompetent and derivative, reproducing the very ideologies that teachers seek to expose (see Buckingham, 2003 for an extended account of this). But such pessimistic attitudes have largely been replaced in more recent years by positive accounts of the value of production work, based in rationales of conceptual learning, creative transformation, and cultural practices of media production increasingly typical of young people's informal media cultures (Potter, 2005; Jenkins, 2006; McDougall, 2006).

The fourth pattern: media texts as poor relations of literature

Finally, successive versions of the English curriculum have demonstrated a suspicion of semiotic modes beyond language. Recent versions recognise the growing argument for a multimodal approach to textuality and literacy (Kress and van Leeuwen, 2000; Jewitt and Kress, 2003); but the occasional reference to multimodal texts arguably produces only internal contradictions within a conservative ring-fencing of language, buttressed by an increasingly unconvincing argument for language's superiority over other communicative modes.

This argument takes curious turns. In 2004-5 a 'conversation' was initiated with stakeholders by the Qualifications and Curriculum Authority, the government agency then responsible for curriculum development, about the future of the English curriculum. In its response document, the QCA argued, in reply to a number of submissions making the case for a version of the curriculum incorporating contemporary media texts, that:

> *Alongside views that media and screen-based texts [can] have their place in English 21 there is the caveat that these should never be at the expense of our rich book-based literary heritage – a point more fully elaborated in terms of the purpose and value of engaging with verbal language: the study of literature has one conspicuous advantage over the study of film and television media, in that it develops the skills of analysis, argument and discourse alongside language skills.* (Qualifications and Curriculum Authority, 2005)

This position can be seen as a diluted residue of Leavis's attack on popular culture. The authors of the curriculum here display a softened stance on the teaching of texts such as comics, films and television, allowing them a place as part of a wider cultural landscape; but there remains the firm belief that they need to be treated suspiciously, and to be seen as somehow thinner, more insubstantial, less nourishing than literature.

This booklet will oppose the 'poor relation' view of media texts, by argument and example. There is no logical reason why the study of comic strip and animated film, for example, should not develop 'the skills of analysis, argument and discourse alongside language skills' just as effectively as the study of classic literature.

3 Media education in the UK: a brief history

The four patterns sketched in the previous chapter are revealed in the long history of media education in the UK. This history is ably summarised by Buckingham (2003: 6-9), to which I refer readers for an extended overview of histories, models, theories and pedagogies. Buckingham detects three phases in his history.

Phase one

The first, Buckingham calls 'Discrimination'. This phase is typified by Leavis, whose continuation of Matthew Arnold's project of culture and civilisation is often cited as the beginning of media education. As noted in the previous chapter, its project was to inculcate a profound mistrust of the mass media, and a consequent appreciation of the values of the literary canon, Leavis's 'Great Tradition' (Leavis, 1948).

Phase two

Buckingham terms his second phase 'Cultural Studies and the Popular Arts', arguing that media education was influenced in the 1960s and 1970s by the new academic discipline of Cultural Studies, represented by the Birmingham Centre for Contemporary Cultural Studies. Under this influence, popular culture came to be seen largely as a positive force, a legitimate part of the 'common culture' described by Raymond Williams (1961). Buckingham associates this phase with Stuart Hall's and Paddy Whannel's book *The Popular Arts* (1965), suggesting that, while the book takes popular culture more seriously, it still expresses reservations about the nature of commercial culture, maintaining that it is media education's role to develop a degree of critical discrimination in school students.

Phase three

The third phase in Buckingham's scheme is 'Screen education and demystification'. Here, he identifies in particular the influence of the British film journal *Screen*, and its exploration of new approaches to textual analysis, in particular semiotics and psychoanalytic theory. He proposes Len Masterman (for example, 1980) as the arch-exponent of this approach, adapting semiotic analysis for classroom use, encouraging teachers and students to expose the workings of dominant ideologies. While Masterman has been, and remains, an inspirational force in the development of media education internationally, Buckingham critiques aspects of his work as politically defensive.

A history of defensiveness

Buckingham's argument is that all three of these phases involve certain kinds of defensiveness against mass culture; and furthermore that the history of media education internationally is notable for – indeed, often begins from – defensive attitudes towards the media, which he sees as falling into three types: cultural defensiveness, moral defensiveness, and political defensiveness.

His own project has been to find a more nuanced approach. This takes its cue partly from Cultural Studies. In a seminal study Buckingham undertook with Julian Sefton-Green, *Cultural Studies Goes to School: Reading and Teaching Popular Media* (Buckingham and Sefton-Green, 1994), the authors make the case for a more positive view of young people's cultural tastes. At the same time, they are careful to distance themselves from more celebratory accounts of young people's media cultures, arguing that media education does have a role in introducing a critical perspective.

Connections with the sociology of childhood and with literacy

Buckingham's work has made two other productive associations: with the debates in literacy education; and with the new sociology of childhood. The former is a component of his work on media education in schools, and of his discussions of media literacy, which he defines as the outcome of media education. This is a key definition of the two terms, which I shall use in the rest of the booklet.

The sociology-of-childhood association characterises Buckingham's research into how younger children watch television, respond to advertising, and make use of computer games and associated products such as Pokémon. The connections with literacy and learning theory lay a valuable foundation for one of the most neglected areas of media education: the primary sector. A connection between childhood studies and literacy practices in education can be seen in the work of primary-school literacy specialists such as Jackie Marsh (for example, Marsh and Larson, 2005), who explore how popular culture and media can be taken seriously in an expanded vision of the literacy curriculum in primary schools.

The British Film Institute

Buckingham's account, and his own work, can be complemented by other threads in the recent history of media education in the UK. One such thread centres on the work of the British Film Institute, whose education section has worked for over two decades to develop resources and curricular frameworks for the teaching of screen media, and to advocate film and media education in the policy domain. The BFI's work has been closely associated with that of other media educators, in co-publishing (Buckingham and Bazalgette, 1995), in co-researching (Reid, Burn and Parker, 2002; Burn and Parker, 2003; Bearne and Bazalgette, 2010; Reid, Burn and Wall, 2013), and in jointly delivering training for teachers.

At the same time, the work of the BFI can be seen in a wider European context, where education in national film heritages is an important component of media education in many countries. This emphasis can be seen as a challenge to some other impulses of media education, in privileging the medium of film over other media and in valuing a national film heritage over popular cinema. However, it can also be seen as a valuable complement to the other impulses, which raises important questions.

Key questions

The situation as described so far provokes a number of key questions.

Is the media curriculum too baggy?

A first question is a challenge to the 'bagginess' of the media curriculum. Can we – do we ever – teach a subject in which all media are evenly represented? Can the teaching of adult newspapers really make connections in the minds of students with the pleasures and conventions of Massively Multiplayer Online Role-playing Games?

Are some media texts more valuable than others?

A second question concerns cultural value. The conventional position in Cultural Studies is to relativise value, and locate it exclusively in the realm of cultural taste, in which the popular cultural affiliations of ordinary people are emphasised. However, while the social formation of cultural preferences is undoubtedly an important aspect of audience engagement with the media, the question of whether cultural judgements around particular texts – are art films more valuable than action movies? is a D. H. Lawrence novel more valuable than a Stephen King novel? are Philip Pullman's books 'better' than J.K. Rowling's books? – in some way respond to objective qualities of the texts themselves remains unsettled; and this emphasis on the qualities of texts is certainly more typical of film education than of other areas of media education.

Who decides on value?

A third unsettled question concerns whether one group's cultural tastes are as legitimate as another's. For some versions of Cultural Studies, the question is settled: popular cultural tastes are championed; 'high' cultural tastes are condemned as elite. While this championing is still undoubtedly a strength of media education – often the only defender of popular culture in curricula still dominated by the values of the traditional arts – film education does remind us that cultural value is a difficult question with no simple answers.

Where should teachers stand?

As teachers negotiate the slippery territory between different cultural allegiances and different kinds of claim to cultural value, they may often need to 'inhabit the paradox', in the words of cultural theorist Steve Connor (1992). In plain speech, this may come down to developing a sensitivity to their students' tastes, pleasures and experience, rather than imposing their own; but also looking for ways to build on students' experiences, introducing them to new texts, new practices, and new ways to manage critical judgement.

Media literacy

An important element in recent developments in media education in the UK has been the explosion of debate about media literacy since the beginning of this century. While versions of the debate exist in many countries, the UK's version began with a statutory responsibility given to the new media super-regulator OFCOM (Office for Communications) to promote media literacy. The discussions initiated by OFCOM's processes of consultation, research and advocacy have been interesting. The definition of media literacy it adopted (Access, Understand, Create) is notable for its recognition of the creative process of media production by ordinary people; but also, less positively, for its omission of the word 'cultural', which is, by contrast, emphasised by advocates of media literacy elsewhere in the UK.

The debate about media literacy is also connected to a pan-European initiative led by a unit in the European Commission, which has developed policy statements about media literacy adopted by the European Parliament and Council of Ministers.

The effect of all this high-level policy-making on schools in the UK has arguably been negligible. Nevertheless, media literacy, and consequently media education, are well established on the European policy agenda, and gaining currency as an important aspect of preparing young people for fulfilling lives in the early 21st century.

Associations of media educators

A final, important initiative to note is the founding in 2007 of a Media Education Association for England and Wales. Scotland has long had its own association, AMES (Association for Media Education in Scotland), but England and Wales have never had their own association until recently. This initiative can be related in various ways to other aspects of the media-education picture in the UK. Unlike the top-down policy process initiated by OFCOM, the associations are in many ways grass-roots phenomena. They emerge from the long history of media education in the UK, and their prominent members are a mix of long-standing practitioners and advocates of media teaching, and younger teachers at the cutting edge of new kinds of practice.

At the same time, the associations have connections with other organisations: some members have been active in the National Association for the Teaching of English, some in the United Kingdom Literacy Association, and these connections represent the related concerns of media teaching and literacy education more generally, as well as the structural interconnections of these domains in the school curriculum.

Current structures and practices

From a more practical point of view, the history and current state of media education in the UK is represented in curricular provision and take-up. Across the four nations and regions, there have been specialist publicly examined media courses in secondary schools since the late 1960s. These specialist courses have traditionally provided the concentrated models of media education, elaborated through examination syllabuses, training procedures and assessment mechanisms, which are a staple element of the kind of media education for which the UK is known, and which are markedly different from other models to be found internationally, especially in Europe and the US (though more similar models exist in Canada, Australia and New Zealand).

In Scotland, which has its own curriculum, the Curriculum for Excellence, there is provision for moving-image education within English. Furthermore, Scotland has a specific evaluation system as part of its sampling of school achievement, which measures progression in learning in respect of moving-image analysis.

In Northern Ireland, media education is located in the curriculum known as the 'Wider Literacy' initiative, which states that its screen education comprises a strategy:

> ...*to embed the use of moving image and related digital technologies across the formal and non-formal curriculum in Northern Ireland.* (Northern Ireland Screen, 2004)

This is a combination of screen and film education with a digital-literacy programme devised in conjunction with the British Film Institute.

Below the age of 14, provision in England and Wales has always been much weaker. Like drama, media education has existed in various versions of the National Curriculum as a sub-set of English, where, significantly, it has been located within the reading component. So, while it has at times been mandatory for (some) schools in England to teach students how to 'read', or analyse, media texts, there has been no requirement to 'write', or make them. Apart from anything else, this position has been inconsistent with OFCOM's statutory responsibility to promote the creation of media texts alongside the critical understanding of them.

The disappearance of media from the new National Curriculum for English

In the primary curriculum, media education has been even more weakly represented than in the first three years of secondary education. Moreover, in the new version of the National Curriculum for English in England, statutory as from September 2014 or September 2015 (Department for Education, 2014), media has been effectively erased from all four Key Stages. This can only be seen as a politically motivated act by a Conservative-led government. Its inclinations can be deduced from the report it commissioned into Cultural Education (Department for Culture, Media and Sport, 2012), which rehearsed the case for the arts in education, with a heavy emphasis on the existing National Curriculum foundation subjects, Art and Music, a brief consideration of the merits of Drama and Dance as independent subjects (subsequently ignored by the government), and a lengthy set of proposals for extra-mural activities to cover the other art forms. These activities included film education; but the word 'media' and the phrases 'media studies' and 'media education' were conspicuously absent from the report. No wonder that the most recent version of the National Curriculum for English should have completed the disappearing act so comprehensively.

There exists, then, no core entitlement for media education for all children; and, in England, no provision at all below Key Stage 4 and GCSE. The rest of this booklet will attempt to recover some of the ground that has been lost. It will consider what the traditions, practices and theories of media education might have to offer an English curriculum to move both English and media education away from the limitations and distortions outlined in the last two chapters. It will propose a comprehensive provision for media education within English from 3 to 16.

4 A model for media education

This chapter offers a model for media education, illustrated by examples, that can underpin work across the age range.

Media and English have been kissing cousins ever since Leavis's launch of what has since been dubbed the 'inoculation' approach to media: the development of critical close reading skills in school students to protect them from the ill effects of the mass media (Leavis and Thompson, 1933/1977). We have seen the three kinds of protectionism in the history of media education which Buckingham (2003) has identified: Leavis's cultural protectionism; the attempt of radical pedagogy in the 1970s and 1980s to protect children from the ideological effects of the media; and the moral protectionism which Buckingham associates more with media education in America.

Let the cousins continue to kiss

Most media teachers in the UK would not now subscribe to any form of protectionism, taking instead a positive view of young people's media cultures and practices, not least because of a general shift towards forms of creative production enabled by the increasing availability of digital authoring tools. However, they would see themselves as teaching forms of critical awareness. In this chapter, I will focus on three aspects of media education which can inform English. It's important not to produce neat models of media education – media studies, for instance – which emphasise difference from, even incompatibility with, English. Such models lead to media as a tacked-on appendage to the English curriculum, at best. More productive, maybe, is to muddle the boundaries, find common ground, and use tensions to challenge each field of study to move beyond its limitations and prejudices.

The three areas I will focus on are *cultural distinction, rhetoric and poetics* and *creative production*. They roughly correspond to key concepts in the English curriculum as identified by the Qualifications and Curriculum Authority (2007): cultural understanding, critical understanding, and creativity. However, my emphasis here will be on the development of media literacy, which is also often understood in terms of this '3Cs' model (Bazalgette, 2008; Burn and Durran, 2007). In my model, a 'CRC' model, the concepts are rather differently understood, in ways which can usefully inform English teaching.

Cultural distinction

The simple way to state the problem here is to say that the English curriculum has traditionally been concerned with 'high' culture (though of course those teachers who come under the category identified in the Cox Report [1989] as 'cultural analysts' have always contested the literary canon and the values associated with it); meanwhile, media education is committed to popular culture (though those who emphasise the importance of film sometimes observe their own kind of canon).

However, the curriculum, oddly, renders the question of culture pretty well invisible. A search through versions of the National Curriculum for English for references to 'culture' or 'cultural' reveals only rather tokenistic references to multiculturalism, as if culture only becomes visible through contrast between ethnic groups. Contrasts between the cultures of different social classes, which might be expected to reveal something of the tension between popular and elite cultural forms and preferences, are not available as a mode of inquiry in the English curriculum. We are enjoined to consider, in short, the meaning of Sujata Bhatt's bilingual tongue, split between English and Gujarati (and see chapter 5 for an example of media-inspired work on this poem); but not to consider why some teenagers might prefer Marvel comics to Shakespeare, *Call of Duty: Modern Warfare* to the war poets, or *Hollyoaks* to Keats. Such contrasts run the risk of reducing the argument to tabloid knockabout of the

'Shakespeare or soaps?' variety, a hoary debate we have had many times before. Nevertheless, it seems important to acknowledge that these kinds of cultural distinction still exist, and to consider how to approach them in the classroom. In any case, my argument is that we don't need to choose. We can, and should, have both extremes of the cultural spectrum, and anything in between that suits our purpose and our students' interests.

Raymond Williams' three levels of culture

The ideas of culture which I have found most helpful in scoping out the cultural space of English and media education are those of Raymond Williams, who identified three levels: *lived culture*, the *documentary record*, and *the selective tradition* (Williams, 1961).

Lived culture was the culture of everyday life, of ordinary people: in effect, a recognition of the vitality of the forms of popular culture which Leavis's approach had represented as debased. Williams recognised the importance of popular music, film, television drama and radio as important parts of this culture, resources to which ordinary people looked for meaning, identity and community, for pleasure, information and entertainment. It is this conception of 'common culture' which has been so influential in the field of Cultural Studies which Williams effectively founded; and which has profoundly informed the conception of popular culture in media studies and media education.

Williams' *documentary record* is the residue of past cultures, inaccessible to us now except through the texts, artefacts and buildings left behind. While Williams' example of ancient Greece is at an extreme distance, we might consider how the media texts of the mid-twentieth century could be viewed by students as documentary records of the spectacular sub-cultures of the fifties and sixties, the political and social significance of punk, the post-colonial cultures of diaspora, or the paranoia of the Cold War. At a greater historical remove, we can consider how the popular cultural texts of modern mass media continue in certain ways the narrative threads, styles, imagery and voices of older popular cultural forms: from the oral tradition of Old English poetry and the mediaeval ballad, through vernacular theatre such as the mystery plays, to the broadsheet ballads, penny dreadfuls and melodramas of the eighteenth and nineteenth centuries. While the popular culture of the modern mass media is different in certain ways, particularly in the production regimes out of which it emerges, in other ways these older textual forms and traditions are the direct ancestors of the modern pop lyric, soap opera, horror film and some genres of computer game.

Finally, Williams' *selective tradition* is the historical process which sifts out some cultural phenomena as more valuable, important, worthy of preservation. It is the process which creates the literary canon, Leavis's Great Tradition. But what we can take from Williams is not the exclusive endorsement of this level of culture above all others, which was the stance adopted by Leavis (and by successive versions of the National Curriculum for English). Rather, we can interrogate with students the processes by which such texts become valued in this way. Through what mechanisms of commentary, critique, transformation, myth-making, appreciation, did Shakespeare become 'greater' than Marlowe or Ben Jonson? Through what kinds of cultural alchemy did low-budget formula movies like *Casablanca* and *Psycho* become elevated into paramount exemplars of cinematic art? These questions of cultural distinction are not ones which the English curriculum prompts, even allows us to ask. Interestingly, though, they're not questions prompted by media education either. Both domains duck the question of cultural value, though both are locked solidly into it. Williams' clear-sighted model offers us a way to think about it constructively.

Three levels of culture: *Beowulf* as a teaching example

What might any of this mean in practice? Let's take, as an example, *Beowulf*. An unquestionably canonical text, the best known of a small surviving group of Old English poems, *Beowulf* is lent value by academic commentary and translated by, amongst others, J.R.R. Tolkien and Seamus Heaney. The poem also usefully highlights the problem of how we define literature. It was orally composed and transmitted before a version was committed to written form, is by no known author, and conforms to Walter Ong's model of oral narrative (Ong, 1982). In particular, the figure of Beowulf himself is what Ong called a 'heavy hero', characterised by a few simple, memorable qualities: agonistic (solving problems through physical action rather than psychological effort) and formulaic, as might be expected in a text strongly influenced by the oral-formulaic process (Parry, 1930; Lord, 1960).

My point in drawing attention to these characteristics is to show that *Beowulf* is in many ways what we now think of as a popular cultural text. This strong, formulaic narrative, in which a mighty hero battles fantasy monsters, may be the earliest jewel in the crown of English literature, performed in the mead-halls of kings as well as for the common folk; but it resembles the adventures of Spiderman, Superman and Batman more than it resembles the tortured protagonists of Renaissance drama or the modern novel. This is not to dismiss the psychological insights, descriptive power, social critique and aesthetic innovation that the prose and poetry of the Renaissance and the modern era produce. My argument is not to prefer the archaic and fantastic over the modern and naturalistic; again, we can have both. I do want, though, to recall vital cultural forms that may get less attention than they deserve at present, and to point out the lineage which links them with modern mediated popular cultural forms, a lineage we can exploit for the benefit of our students.

In this respect, we can consider what happens when a text like this is adapted into a contemporary media form. *Beowulf* was produced as an animated film in 2007 (Zemeckis, 2007). In comic-book style, scripted by the graphic novelist Neil Gaiman, it represented Beowulf as a muscled super-hero (voiced with Cockney bravado by Ray Winstone) and Grendel's mother as a naked temptress (Angelina Jolie). The popular cultural references to comic-strip narrative and fantasy film will have made a connection with the imaginative worlds and media cultures of many students in our classrooms. But this connection is not contrived, superficial or gratuitous. The point of the *Beowulf* movie for the English and media teacher is that it is an example of the continuity of popular narrative, of how its tropes, structures, values and affective charge descend in a discernible line from the archaic worlds of Achilles and Beowulf to the superheroes of Marvel comics. It is the line of descent that can be traced through the transformative threads which take Arthur and the Matter of Britain from early mediaeval verse through Malory's great prose epic to Tennyson's mournful idylls, T.H. White's comic genius, and the profusion of Arthurian film, animation and television dramas of the late twentieth century. It is the narrative simplicity and demotic appeal of Robin Hood, utterly transformed yet completely unchanged in his journey from mediaeval ballad cycle to the competing film icons of Errol Flynn, Sean Connery, Kevin Costner and Russell Crowe.

There are plenty of lessons here for the English and media classroom about the form and content of popular cultural narrative. What do superheroes mean, and why are they perennially fascinating to us? What serious themes do they enact, of justice, identity, freedom, revenge, gendered power, behind their fantastic costumes and elaborate weaponry, from Beowulf's sword to Batman's utility belt, Athena's shield to Xena's spinning steel ring? How are these meanings encoded in the poetic forms of successive ages, from alliterative verse and kenning to the chiaroscuro of late twentieth-century comic-book art, or the rapid editing, CGI effects and condensed scripting of superhero film franchises? These are questions about meaning and representation; but also about semiotic mode and medium.

There are serious questions here about the nature of culture, distinctions between differently valued cultural forms, and the articulation between such texts and the cultural lives of our students. These are questions about which the pedagogies and curricula of English and media remain routinely dumb, each content to outlaw the cultural territory of the other, and defend the values of its own terrain. This is not a matter of wilful choice by today's teachers, but of sedimented practice accreted over time, and regressive curriculum policy.

Let's move on, however, and look at the relatively new medium of computer games. The animated film of *Beowulf* has been further adapted into a computer game version (*Beowulf*, 2007). Game versions have been developed in many cross-media franchises of interest to the English and media classroom: for example, *The Lord of the Rings*, the *Harry Potter* stories, and the film based on the first of Philip Pullman's *Northern Lights* sequence (where you can wield a Wii-mote and nunchuk as an armoured bear). I'll come back to how computer games might help us think in different ways about narrative, language and literacy. Here, the focus is on their cultural status and function.

An argument for English teachers to consider is that computer games are particularly well suited to adapt the ancient narratives of oral tradition I have described above. This is partly because they share the popular cultural milieu of their sister media forms. But it is also because they are, literally, formulaic texts, made up of computer code. Suppose you want to describe the death of a warrior in battle. The sensibility of modern literature requires variety and originality. Cliché and formula are the enemies. We need different words to describe the warrior's fall each time; different words to describe the sounds of battle; novel ways to render the agony of death.

For Homeric texts, the opposite was true. The oral poet, performer and audience needed the repetition of the same words for these familiar scenarios: words that could be easily remembered, easily re-ordered if the performer needed to alter the narrative, and easily recognised by an audience which needed familiar stories. The battlefield slaughter of *The Iliad* follows a well-rehearsed formula of weapon use, disembowelling and the ringing of armour about the fallen warrior. The computer game is not dissimilar. The character is a bundle of audiovisual resources, constant through the game. The actions of killing an enemy will involve triggering the same animation cycle, the same soundtrack, the same range of player options each time. As in the oral performance, significant variations on the theme are possible, such as the way in which these options can be exercised by the player. Although computer games are very different from traditional oral narratives in many ways, both employ formulaic narrative techniques, integral components of the popular aesthetic.

Finally, while popular culture is more than able to explore the serious preoccupations of everyday life, we always know that the fictions we love to spin about these concerns are a kind of game. When we enter Coleridge's 'willing suspension of disbelief', it is very similar to entering the contract about the status of a game: that however dramatic the combat, claws will be sheathed; however convincing the representation, its rules only apply within the magic circle of the game, as the influential play scholar Johan Huizinga (1949) described it. Above all, the game is played for pleasure, a fact never adequately represented in curricular programmes. It is important to consider how such pleasures may fall into different categories, perform different psycho-social roles: the thrill of risk for a teenager aspiring to adulthood; the pleasure of catharsis in tragic narratives; the pleasure of humorous, subversive, carnivalesque inversions of officialdom (or, for children, of the adult world).

A sensibility which connects the oral culture which produced Beowulf to the performative, improvisatory dynamic of the video game, then, might have much to offer the cultural work of the English and media classroom: a recuperation of ancient stories, styles and values; a dramatic engagement for students with the protagonists of these narratives; a goal-oriented approach to the problems of everyday life; and a reminder of the importance of pleasure and play.

Rhetoric and poetics

English and media education have quite different approaches to the characteristics of texts. Approaches to literary texts have often focused on their aesthetic form, and have been characterised by what we might call a mode of appreciation, a poetical mode. By contrast, media texts have been approached in what we might call a rhetorical mode, exploring the politics of representation, and interrogating the motivations of producers and audiences.

These two modes have long histories which can be traced back to Aristotle: we can detect the legacy of his *Poetics* in the English approach to literature, and the legacy of his *Rhetoric* in the media approach to the texts that fall within its domain. I simplify here for the sake of contrast; but, both in the habituated practices of the English and media classrooms, and in the curricular formations that have constructed literature as an object of reverence and media texts as objects of suspicion, something like this contrast seems stubbornly resistant to change. We need both rhetoric and poetics if we are to attend to the politics of representation in both media and literary texts, as well as to the aesthetic forms in which such representations are framed. Indeed, these should not be alternative, incompatible ways of looking at culture, but indivisible: two sides of the same coin. All rhetoric operates through aesthetic form and claims aesthetic value; all aesthetic form has a rhetorical, even political, purpose.

The rhetorical stance of media education is often encoded in the conceptual frameworks used to identify what critical understandings students might be expected to gain. There are several different versions of these, but they can generally be grouped under *institutions*, *texts* and *audiences*.

Institutions

The idea of media institutions is a staple of media education. It is rarely considered in the teaching of literature, though much of Dickens' work was structured by the contingencies of magazine publication, though the careers of the women writers of the 19th century were at the mercy of male publishers, and though the literary creations of modern novelists are commonly franchised by multinational media organisations. To move beyond the immediate pleasures of engagement with media texts in order to consider the shadowy regimes of production and distribution that lie behind them can seem dry, remote and hard to pin down. There are also uncertainties: what institutions are we talking about exactly? what do we need to know about them? why do we need to know it?

Current approaches to media education would support a nuanced attitude to the question of the media industries. Buckingham (1998) argues, for instance, that we have moved beyond a paradigm of 'radical pedagogy' in which the role of education is to unmask bourgeois and capitalist ideologies. This is not to say that a degree of healthy scepticism is not warranted. There are good reasons why we might want young people to understand what commercial interests lie behind a MacDonalds advert or a leader in a Murdoch- or Rothermere-owned newspaper. But institutions more typically have complex motives and socio-political functions. The practical question is: how might we explore these?

In one primary-school example, to a version of which – adapted for use in a secondary classroom – we will return in the next chapter, a colleague explored the cross-media *Harry Potter* franchise by looking at logos on the covers of the book, the DVD box and the game box. The media institutions involved included Bloomsbury, Sony, Knowwonder games, Electronic Arts, the *Times Educational Supplement*, Dolby sound, and several more. The complexity of function speaks for itself. Some institutional functions are familiar, yet opaque. The age-rating of both films and games, for example, is familiar to the students; but they have little knowledge of the institutions that create these regulatory constraints which affect their viewing and play. The logos of the BBFC (British Board of Film Classification) and PEGI (Pan-European Game Information), which determine age-rating for films and games respectively, prompt the students to explore these institutions and their different motivations: one is a public body, the other an industry-created system.

Another example comes from a Year 4 primary classroom where the activity involved researching the BBC. When the teacher asks, 'Does anybody know how the BBC gets its money?', some children begin to use previously acquired knowledge to help them speculate. There are no adverts on the BBC so it's not like Sky. Jamie speculates that the audiences have to pay for the channels they watch and seems to be drawing from experience of subscription channels. The children are beginning to generalise from their own experience of the media, even if this produces the wrong conclusion. The teacher asks, 'Do you have to pay to get the BBC?' Odette says no, it's always been there. She is surprised when the teacher provides information about the licence fee. This evidence of partial understanding of media economics shows how children theorise from their experience; and how they amend their ideas with new information.

Texts

A rhetorical approach to texts will centre on the question of *representation*. This is a familiar word in media education and media studies; not so commonly found in English documents or conceptual frameworks. At one level, of course, representation means any semiotic act: any utterance, written word, image, dramatic gesture, is a representation of some aspect of reality. The question to explore with students is the nature of the relationship between the representation and that 'reality', which is multiple, shifting and situated. We may explore Shylock as a representation of Renaissance ideas about Jewishness; but we cannot escape the fact that the actor depicting the role, the director behind him, and the audience in the theatre (or cinema) have more recent memories of the Holocaust and the Arab-Israeli conflict. To return to the example of *Beowulf*, we might investigate how the character represents an ideal of the Anglo-Saxon warrior prince. But we can also attend to the meanings of the contemporary superhero which the animated film invokes; or to the gendered significance of the combat mechanics in the computer game.

How, though, might students understand the detailed structure of texts which produce these meanings?

One approach is to focus on the signifying systems of particular media. Here is an example from film. A Year 8 boy is writing about what he has learnt from re-editing a sequence from Baz Luhrmann's *Romeo + Juliet* (1996). His task was to take a sequence of footage from the film, imported into the editing software Adobe Premiere, and to creatively rework it, adding different music, changing the order and duration, producing his own take on the play using these 'found' resources.

> *Also, at that point when the camera tracks up, it is the first time there has been any significant movement in it. The camera has stayed still to reflect the movement of the most important character in the sequence: like Mercutio, the camera has witnessed everything, but has done nothing about it... The final shot is of a new character to the sequence: Sampson. The camera is placed at an oblique angle to him. He is not an important character, he is at the side of the action. His emotion, his expression of fear and anxiety, needs to be acknowledged – not felt – by the audience. He simply watches – he does not act.* (Josh)

This kind of critical work, a fluid mix of technical production, aesthetic choices and critical reflection, is close to the kind of work a student might undertake in analysing literature. Media teachers would recognise it as a thoughtful reading of a filmic text, aware of both the grammar of the moving image and the meanings conveyed by it. English teachers would recognise it as an equally thoughtful reading of a sequence from *Romeo and Juliet*. It can be seen as an aspect of critical literacy, and as situated within the conceptual framework of media education. But it also exemplifies the kind of thing I am thinking of as a 'poetics' of media education: an attention to the aesthetic features of dramatic texts which Aristotle codified, adapted for the photographic media of the early 21st century.

In this example, work in different media extends the understanding of textual structures that students might learn in English. To the metalinguistic lexicon of clause, sentence, paragraph, narrative, argument and so on is added the grammar of film (shots, camera movement, camera angle).

However, these new understandings are not simply additive: they can be mutually reinforcing. An English teacher in a recent media-literacy project asked Year 8 students to think about systems of address across book, game and film, first in relation to *Harry Potter*, then through making their own stories, films and games. In doing so, the students' understanding of a complex set of ideas such as point-of-view, person, address, focalisation (Genette, 1980) became richer, more robust, less susceptible to reductive formulations. Such semiotic principles run across different modes and media: they are, in short, multimodal (Kress and van Leeuwen, 2000).

Attention to the representational strategies and the poetics of texts can be reinforced, enriched, made more complex if it encompasses the semiotic structures of different media.

Another example comes from a Year 3 primary classroom, where the group is studying newspapers, and making their own. The children have analysed a series of front-page headlines, looking at how they condense the narrative into a few words, how they give clues to the reader about the importance and meaning of the story, and how they use language in memorable and unusual ways. When they move on to making their own front pages, they put this new knowledge to good use. One child uses a pun for his headline about recent bad weather in the school's local area: 'Snow Way!' The children had recently learned about the efficiency and humour of puns, and the use of punctuation in headlines for emphasis, and Jamie was putting his newly acquired knowledge to work in a different context.

This example demonstrates the importance of keeping the rhetoric and poetics of the media closely linked, two sides of the same coin. The analysis and production of news media inevitably foregrounds rhetorical functions – exploring texts which persuade, inform, entertain – but they can accomplish this through the study and use of linguistic features which are essentially the ones which poets also deploy.

Audience

It is now orthodox for English teachers and media teachers to encourage students to create texts for a particular audience. But who that audience might be, or how we might get a concrete idea of her, him or them, is a slippery business. We can imagine, for instance, a series of concentric circles, the innermost of which is the students themselves. What are their reading/viewing/playing preferences? How do they make particular cultural choices? What kinds of pleasure do they derive from the texts they choose? In what social groups do they engage with these texts? What cultural practices do they engage in as audiences? The next circle outward might be a specific other audience, involving making texts for a partner primary-school class, for a parents' evening, for a local council meeting, for a visiting VIP. The outermost circle, one often used by media teachers, could be the socio-economic groupings of market research: are the students targeting their texts at the A1 or the C2 grouping, for example?

This kind of differentiation of audiences can be seen in a project in which Year 4 children devise their own media campaign to promote health awareness in the face of a (fictional) virus. To research their own health advertising campaign, the class watches a range of public health advertisements, and speculates about audience responses. 'Too much information bores people, too much scary stuff puts them off,' one group decides. The children are differentiating between audience reactions. Watching flu adverts, the class becomes aware of their own visceral reactions to the ads: the groans, moans and 'yuks'. They sing along with the catchy refrain from a swine flu advert, 'Catch it, bin it, kill it', punching their arms in the air. They have begun their audience research with themselves, recognising that audience pleasure is as important as the factual message of the advert. As a further part of the research, two children interview dinner ladies, who are emphatic about the importance of health measures in schools and families. The children realise that audiences different from themselves may have different interests, which they will need to address in their campaign.

A group of three interviews the school secretary to prepare for their public health campaign. The interviewers are surprised when she says she has no TV. They consider the value of different media, including radio and the internet. They have learnt something about the importance of audience media preferences.

Students need regularly to consider a diversity of audiences if they are to learn how texts are adopted or rejected, how cultural affiliations are made and broken, how meanings are interpreted, how cultural resources are appropriated and transformed, what pleasures are sought and found, and in what social configurations, for what cultural or political purposes, all this happens.

Analysing audience behaviours is only part of the picture, however. Let us not forget effect. Do we really want a world where there are no media 'effects'? Of course we don't want an entire generation uncritically swallowing the message that life without Coke or Playstation isn't worth living. But do we want students to be unmoved by the affective charge of horror or romance; unaffected by the polemic of Orwell's *1984* or Lennon's 'Imagine'; unamused by the satirical humour of *The Simpsons*? The great 19th century French magician, Jean-Eugene Robert-Houdin, argued that he much preferred to perform his illusions to intelligent people than to stupid people. Stupid people would always try to see how the trick was done, thereby making his job more difficult and destroying their own pleasure; while intelligent people would allow themselves to be duped, knowing that this was where the enjoyment of the experience lay. We could make the same argument about the media, while rejecting Robert-Houdin's crude dualism about people. We can know it is an illusion, and still surrender ourselves to its spell. It is the paradox of Coleridge's 'willing suspension of disbelief'.

Creative production

Creativity in education is a highly contested idea, appearing in a bewildering variety of forms (Banaji and Burn with Buckingham, 2007). Here, I draw on the work of the Russian psychologist Lev Vygotsky, for whom the creativity of children and adolescents was closely related to play (Vygotsky 1931/1998). In playful activity, children learn the meaning of symbolic substitution through the manipulation of physical objects: Vygotsky's well known example is a child using a broomstick as an imaginary horse. These symbolic understandings become internalised and develop into the mental processes which generate creative work. For Vygotksy, true creativity only develops, however, when the imaginative transformations of play are connected with thinking in concepts: in other words, with rational intellectual processes.

What might creative production look like in the English and media classroom?

Scary films

In one example, from a Year 2 classroom, six-year-olds are devising their own 'scary films'. They have looked at a range of picture-books and films which exemplify such stories, involving monsters, aliens, and things that go bump in the night. They have discussed the oddness of creating stories which frighten people, and the appeal this holds for audiences. They move on to storyboard, film and edit their own stories. A much-debated point in the discussion is how to convey the sense of fear, and in particular how to show the monsters in their stories.

One group decides to show 'the monster in the library' in its full glory, with two children dressing up in a green cloak with a monster mask. Another group decides, with encouragement from the teacher, that they won't show the monster at all, but will create the sense of the frightening phenomenon entirely through showing the reaction of the victim. In one frame of the children's storyboard, a character has been drawn especially small to communicate vulnerability. The teacher asks how this might be filmed. The children tell him to stand on one of the desks so that he can film the character from a high angle, again representing vulnerability.

These two approaches exemplify aspects of Vygotsky's model of creativity. In the former case, material resources are collected and repurposed to create the visual effect of the monster, much as Vygotsky's broomstick horse is created by children at play. The monster is, however, elaborated through dramatic movement (the children wriggle convincingly across the library floor), and vocal articulation (grunts), so that a more developed narrative is created. This narrative is, in turn, developed further by the filming of the monster and the victim, and the editing which alternately cuts between them, showing the victim's deliciously terrified reactions. The playful imaginative creation of a fantasy figure is subordinated to the logic of narrative structure and meaning.

The second group's decision is rather more complex. To appreciate that an entity in film can be represented by its absence is a step forward; and to imagine a monster only evident through the emotional effects it creates is obviously a step further on from imagining a broomstick to be a horse. Here, the resources involve the dramatic work of the victim, and the use of what Vygotsky calls 'tools', which can be both material and conceptual. In this case, the high-angle filming is the material tool, while the concept of the power imbalance it represents is the conceptual tool. The use of these tools creates the sense of fear visible in the victim; and also creates an implied monster rather than a visible one, which in turn shows the children's understanding of the inferential work of the audience.

Creativity here, then, is by no means a vague, romantic affair, but a specific set of imaginative processes organised by a mixture of signifying systems. The meanings of dramatic action, the grammar of film, the significance of costume and mask, and the emotional (and narrative) meanings of music are all integrated in the children's work.

Machinima

Another example is drawn from a project in which a group of 30 eleven-year-olds make a machinima film. Machinima is perhaps most recent cultural form in the world of animation. The word itself is a portmanteau combining 'machine' and 'cinema', with a substitution of the 'e' by an 'i', implying 'animation' and 'animé'. Machinima is defined by Kelland *et al.* (2005: 10) as 'the art of making animated films within a real-time 3-D environment'. It can be thought of as animation made from the 3-D environments and animated characters of computer games or virtual immersive worlds.

The children's film tells the story of a computer geek called Jeff, who meets an alien character, Dr T, in a videogame, travels with him to Cleopatra's palace, and eventually prevents his evil plan for world domination.

Martha and Rosa are editing the scene in which two characters, Jeff and Dr T, have arrived at Cleopatra's palace, and have to convince her guard to let them in. They are editing to a printed script, which is a transcript of the improvised dialogue of the voice-acting group in the class. They tell me how they will edit a conversation sequence:

> AB: *If you were filming two people talking, how would you do it?*
> R: *You'd put the camera there, and one of them would be there, and one would be there [indicating 'side-by-side' with hands].*
> AB: *What's your other option?*
> R: *You could put the camera on the person talking...*
> M: *And then switch it round.*

Here, Martha and Rosa first suggest a two-shot for a conversation, and move towards the idea of shot-reverse-shot in response to my question. Elsewhere in my conversation with them, they show that they are quite confident about the idea of shot distance and its function of emphasis. They describe kinds of camera movement and the function of low- and high-angle shots to signify power, although these have not been explicitly taught at this stage. When asked how these ideas could apply to their scene, they suggest that Cleopatra and the guard might be filmed from a low angle. When they move on to insert camera angles, they do exactly this. Figure 1 shows the two shots in which Dr T and Jeff meet Cleopatra's guard.

Figure 1: Martha's and Rosa's shot-reverse-shot sequence, with the music track composed by another group

As with the six-year-olds in the previous example, the imaginative processes here which create the characters, the story and the setting are articulated through the grammar of the moving image. The girls editing the sequence in Figure 1 are having to work out how to create the narrative tension in the encounter between Dr T, Jeff and Cleopatra's guard. To do this, they need to employ the familiar shot-reverse-shot sequence of film grammar. However, although in a sense this is 'old news', since it is a formula they view and understand on TV and film most days of their lives, in another sense they are having to create it from new. It is often argued that the continuity editing conventions of film are designed to be invisible, to produce an apparently seamless representation of reality which 'sutures' the viewer into its view. If this is true, it partly explains why, although students read the shot-reverse-shot convention repeatedly in their daily lives, when it comes to making their own films, it's as if they need to repeat a chapter of film-making history, and discover it for themselves. This is creative work: a purposeful planning of how to represent a conversation through multiple point-of-view.

Recursive processes

These examples indicate that creativity, rather than being a kind of mystical divine gift, is something we can be specific about, nurture in particular ways, and evaluate. The examples also give some sense of how learning progression works in media education: it is recursive rather than linear, as the outline curriculum in chapter 6 will propose. In one sense, the six-year-olds in the examples above are doing the same thing as the eleven-year-olds: planning, filming and editing. Yet the examples also make it clear that these processes are becoming increasingly sophisticated, complex, and diverse in their forms of representation, in ways teachers can recognise and build on. They are also multimodal: the example in Figure 1 shows how the girls have incorporated the music track composed and performed by another group. This raises the question of how media teachers might, as well as connecting with English and drama, collaborate more broadly across the arts.

To sum up, then, we can say that creativity in media production builds on playful experiment, and involves:

- imaginative work, bringing images, ideas, stories, sounds into being in ways that are new, innovative, valuable
- the use of and transformation of existing cultural resources – visual, auditory, material
- the use of physical and conceptual tools, many of which are exactly those explored in the rhetorical and poetic work described earlier.

5 More examples of media education in practice

The examples in this chapter are projects which have been undertaken in primary and secondary schools. They have been chosen to represent a range of critical and creative work in a range of different media.

Animation in the primary school

This project was developed with Year 3 children.

The children first discuss the meaning of 'animation'. They watch a short animated film, and then look at how a series of still frames from the film can be run together to create the illusion of movement. They are then introduced to simple animation software which captures a sequence of still photographs through a webcam, and runs them together to make an animation. The children practise animating toys or other objects as smoothly as possible. At this age, they need clear reinforcement of essential concepts and of routines for animating, and there is a need for more demonstration than with older children. However, they find the process accessible and enjoyable. It appears to put production before design; but the advantage of using the production technology first is that the children have a clear idea from practical experience of what this medium can do as they undertake design processes such as storyboarding.

The children's own film is based on the familiar tale of 'The Boy Who Cried Wolf'. The children storyboard their film carefully, working first as a whole class. At this point, they are introduced to notions of moving-image grammar, and have to decide whether portions of the script demand long shots or close-ups, cutaways or reaction shots. Each shot is given a defined length, which is converted into a number of frames. The storyboard is created on A4 sheets, each containing one shot. After the process and the outcomes have been modelled, the class divides into small groups to continue planning the film. Each small group is responsible for designing and animating a small portion of the overall work.

The children then create plasticine models of the characters, and draw the sets on cardboard and paper. Then they film each shot with a cheap webcam. Figure 2 shows one child positioning a model before the shot is taken. The whole process takes three or four hours. The software is easy to learn and to use, and there is little post-production work to do.

Figure 2: Positioning a character model before taking an animation shot

The learning objective of the activity is to help children understand how moving images work. On the table-top, the children are able to construct a range of camera shots, and they quickly and easily acquire a vocabulary with which to describe and analyse these, as they storyboard and translate their ideas into animation:

The [shots] I found most useful were two-shots (with two people), over-shoulder shots (looking over a figure's shoulder at other figures), close-ups and one-shots (one person). (Layla)

First before you make the animation you need to plan it because if you don't it won't work. (Victor)

There is a continual emphasis in the children's discussion on how moving pictures can tell stories, and how the images which the children are creating can best do that.

Comic-strip superheroes

This is a Year 8 media project. It begins with watching and discussing the animated film *Batman and the Mask of the Phantasm* (Radomski and Timm, 1993). The film is presented to students as imitating quite closely the visual style and spirit of the original DC Comics *Batman* cartoons: it derives from a TV series which consciously resurrected the 'Dark Knight' and Art Deco detail of Bob Kane's design in the 1940s.

Before watching, the students are introduced to the idea of *representation*. The teachers draws a figure on the board and asks the students what it is, teasing out the point that this is not a person, but a representation of a person.

As students watch the film, they make notes on four aspects of representation:
- how criminals are represented
- how women are represented
- how the city environment is represented
- the character of Bruce Wayne/Batman.

By adding and changing details in the drawing, ideas about representation can be elicited: representations can be stereotypical or differentiated, positive or negative, realistic or unrealistic; they may be encoded in clothing, or words and actions, or physical arrangements. With this conceptual equipment, students are asked to comment on representations in the film. Criminals are stereotyped as broad-hatted, cigarette-smoking gangsters, or – in the figure of the Joker – made exciting and extraordinary. Women are either shallow and weak, or secretly dynamic and physically powerful. These representations are related in discussion to what students know or can be told of the cultural values and concerns of 1940s America.

This discussion is the groundwork for a close reading of the film, through the analysis of still images. Students are presented with specific stills, chosen for their relevance to the four areas students have been looking at in the film. So, for example, there are two stills in which women are represented, and two in which criminals are represented. Students discuss the images in groups and present their ideas to the rest of the class. To help them, they have some prompt questions, and the teacher also models ways of reading the images. Students are shown how to read meaning into details; they have also to consider some conventions of filmic images: aspects of shot construction such as lighting, camera angle and shot distance.

The film provides an immediate frame of reference for discussing some of the 'ingredients' of a superhero: an alter-ego, powers, gadgets, masks, motivation, the nemesis, exotic imagery. Students then research and compare heroes from myth and legend: Hercules, Robin Hood, Anansi, Mwimbo, William Wallace. The emphasis in subsequent discussion is on how this 20th-century popular-cultural phenomenon might be part of a continuity across history and cultures. What is the universal appeal of such narratives? The question of the representation of gender is also raised: why have superheroes and action heroes been so overwhelmingly male in the past? How is the new wave of female action heroes (Xena, Warrior Princess, Buffy the Vampire Slayer, Lara Croft) different? One aspect of these fantasy characters which appeals to young people can be the symbolic resources the characters offer to help the young people reflect on their own identities: their 'real' selves as well as aspirational versions of themselves which they can construct and experiment with through the making of their own media texts.

Essential to this discussion is a consideration of audience: of what superheroes mean to people, at various levels. In the next activity students focus on the centrally important idea of 'audience pleasure', through close reading of the covers of some superhero comics. Details in the covers promise cathartic action and excitement, ideals of protective power and fantasies of transformation. They offer dystopian reflections of urban menace and promise the utopian triumph of good over evil. Students are encouraged to consider the needs of particular audiences: perhaps the strong but feminine 'Miss Fury', sending a group of suited men flying with well-aimed kicks and punches, provided a fantasy of liberation for young girls in 1950s America; perhaps an image of Batman confronting a top-hatted, cigar-smoking capitalist was an inspiration to post-Depression workers.

Students also look at the 'comic cover' as a genre of its own, finding patterns and listing conventions in the layout and the imagery. This prompts a further development of students' understanding of visual grammar. The framework the teacher has used is borrowed from Kress's and van Leeuwen's *Reading Images: The Grammar of Visual Design* (1996).

Students then design a cover for an invented superhero comic, and – if there is time – they design a page of the comic too. The two examples below show different approaches to these designs. The first (Figure 3), 'The Adventures of Super-Ellen', is a group-created photostory, in which drama skills are integrated with media skills to create the narrative. The second (Figure 4), 'Tigerwoman', is a drawn comic cover by one girl. Both explore the representation of gender in comic-strip superhero narratives.

Figure 3: Super-Ellen: Year 8 photostory design

Figure 4: Tigerwoman: Year 8 superhero comic design

TV hospital dramas

This Year 8 project aims to introduce students to some key ideas about television audiences and scheduling. In terms of the conceptual framework of media education, it requires them to think about both media institutions and media audiences, and the relation between them.

The project also aims to develop students' understanding of genre and narrative structure, and – at a finer level – to develop their understanding of how camera shots are edited together to convey narrative. There is also a practical element: students use video cameras to create a short narrative sequence, learning to edit 'in-camera' and encountering some disciplines of simple video production. Meanwhile, they further develop their ability to structure and sustain complex explanations and analyses in writing.

The hospital drama genre

The project begins with a general discussion of the hospital drama genre. In groups, students make a list of TV programmes that they have watched over the past week, and then try to group them into categories. They discuss how these categories might be identified, and they are introduced – or reintroduced – to the concept of genre. They then use TV listings to identify various genres and subgenres of TV drama. It becomes clear at this point that genres are not simply innate properties of media texts, but are also constructed by media institutions such as production companies, broadcasters and TV listings magazines.

Introduced formally to the idea of *genre elements*, students brainstorm such elements of hospital dramas. Then they start to watch an episode of the UK hospital soap *Casualty*, identifying examples of iconography and of typical characters, settings, narratives and themes. At a basic level, students simply understand that TV dramas can be categorised, and are able to describe these categories. However, they usually display a rich, implicit understanding of these genre elements, and enjoy categorising and naming them more formally. At a more extended level, students apply the concept of iconography more broadly, and begin to understand the importance of recognition and expectation in audiences' relationship with genres.

A drama for children's TV

At this early stage of the project, students are introduced to the longer-term project of inventing a new hospital drama for children's TV and 'pitching' it to CBBC, one of the BBC's digital channels for children. They brainstorm ideas for what might make a good children's hospital drama, and what would appeal to a target audience of children. At ages 12 and 13, the students are still connected enough to this audience to enjoy the imaginative investment, yet their emerging self-image as teenagers gives them enough distance to discuss this audience with (equally pleasurable) objectivity.

To begin the creative process, the students invent titles for their new dramas. First, they examine existing hospital drama titles. What makes them appealing? What linguistic tricks do they employ? What do they connote? In groups, they brainstorm ideas. Subgenres necessarily emerge: for example, emergency-based and ward-based dramas. Students then fix on a title for their own series, and – for homework – begin to create characters and broad situations for them. Creativity here involves the invention of new media representations, but these are clearly linked to a critical exploration of existing representations.

From this point on, the students use spare lesson time and homework to develop their series ideas and their pitches.

Narrative structure

The next stage of the project involves looking more closely at narrative structure. Students are introduced to the idea of three layers of narrative: 'serial' narratives, which carry over from episode to episode; 'episodic' narratives, which are contained within one viewing session; and 'incidental' narratives, which are contained in a short scene or sequence. Continuing to watch the episode of *Casualty*, the students note and discuss examples of each. They discuss how each narrative is incorporated into the episode: its pacing and signalling. How important is each kind of narrative in the episode?

Studying and making a video sequence

The project then focuses on a production activity, in which students make short video sequences, edited in camera. They study a 20-second sequence from *Casualty,* in which a false expectation of an accident is built up through the use of camera shots, and through play on genre expectations. In the sequence a boy ascends a climbing wall, goaded on by another boy, accompanied by a girl who 'can't watch'.

Before they see the sequence, students just listen to the sound track, speculate about what is happening and discuss how tension is developed just by the diegetic sound: sound whose source is visible on the screen or whose source is implied to be present by the action of the film (in *Casualty* there is no helpful mood music). Students are then given the 13 camera shots from the sequence as still images on cards, which they attempt to arrange in order.

Students then view the actual sequence and, in discussion, begin to analyse the shots, making notes on the function of each one within the sequence, and on how it might be formally described. In this instructional part of the lesson, students focus on moving-image grammar. They are revising basic shot types, distances and angles, but the main emphasis is on how shots work in sequence to create the illusion of continuous action in contiguous spaces and time. Meanings are created by juxtapositions: a shot of a boy and girl looking up is 'explained' by a subsequent shot of the climber; a close-up of a hand gripping rock follows a high-angle shot of a climber's frightened face, meaning that he is struggling to hold on; a shot of the climber glancing down means that a subsequent swinging view down the rock face is his point of view. The students learn formal terms to describe grammatical relationships between shots: cut-aways, reaction shots and reverse angles. They also reflect on the significance of camera movement and on the pacing of shots. They then write analytically about the sequence, rehearsing and consolidating their understanding.

Before planning their own sequence, students view examples of work by previous classes: very short tense sequences, of between 10 and 20 seconds, composed usually of between six and ten camera shots. Such brevity is an essential element of the exercise. Of course, it makes the process manageable and containable within the lesson time. More importantly, it enforces a thoughtful distillation of genre and filming conventions. Paradoxically, the students find this liberating: 'The simpler the idea for your sequence, the more you can do with it' (Lisa).

The viewing of these examples is structured carefully. The students notice how the sequences are typical of the hospital drama genre. They are asked to count and time shots. They look at how shots are composed and sequenced to create tension, and how expectations are created and significances signalled. They comment critically on the success of different examples, and speculate about what will have been hard or easy to achieve. They are then ready (and very eager) to make their own (Figure 5).

The teacher organises this activity with the whole class. This is not easy, and it is essential that he or she has already practised. There are management challenges: for example, keeping the whole class engaged (and quiet for shots) when only a few can be actively involved. This difficulty is minimised if the camera is connected to a projector, or just to a TV screen, so that all of the class can 'share' the viewfinder. The student holding the camera is then just doing that: holding the camera. The whole class can join in and collectively own the directing of the shots. The composition of each can be discussed and revised, and it is through this that much of the explicit teaching of visual and moving-image grammar can happen. The sequence is storyboarded quickly – a series of very rough sketches on the whiteboard. The exact framing of each shot is discussed as it is set up.

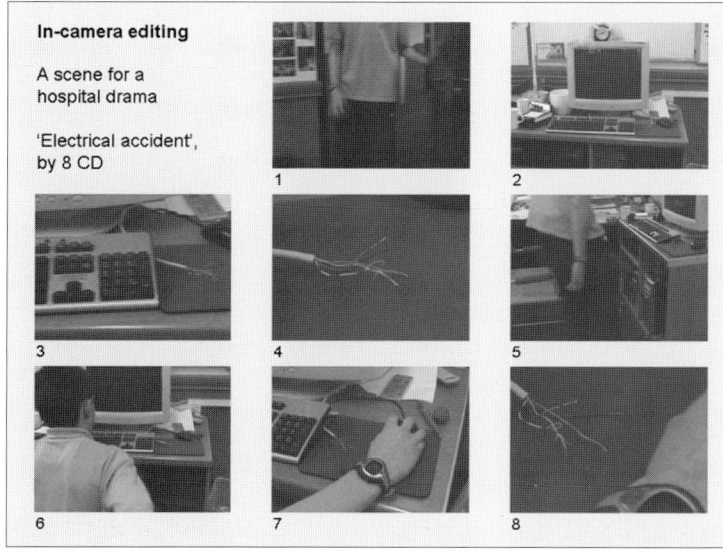

Figure 5: 'Electrical Accident' video sequence

Students then make another sequence, this time working in groups. They spend about half of one 50-minute lesson planning their films: discussing ideas, deciding on a location, sketching a rough storyboard, allocating roles. They then have a lesson (or, if possible a double lesson) to shoot. The films are often dramatisations of specific peer-cultural concerns: teenage risk-taking, bullying, conflict between factions, rebellious behaviour. Other popular themes (as in Figure 6) are more straightforward 'accidents', such as tripping on stairs or picking up a faulty appliance.

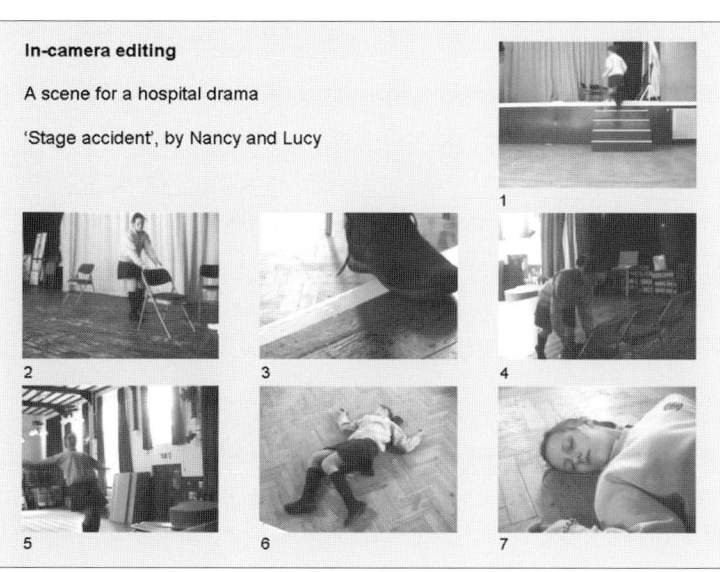

Figure 6: 'Stage Accident' video sequence

Critical reflection is an essential part of the process. Either as a class or in groups, students view their films and consider how they could be improved. Groups can watch their films on the cameras' flip-out screens, but it is better if the footage can be quickly uploaded to a computer as a movie file. In this format, it is much easier for a group to view the sequence critically, moving backwards and forwards fluently to analyse edits and to check continuity. Groups' second attempts are invariably much better – more precisely edited and better constructed for meaning.

Essential to the whole exercise is students' developing sense of the grammar of moving-image sequences:

> *...we used more inventive angles and distances.* (Jenny)
>
> *...we added an extra close-up...* (Ellen)

The process prompts sophisticated thinking about the way sequenced camera shots tell a story, create mood and control tension:

> *At the end of our sequence, instead of focusing on the injured, we had a close-up of feet from the side running up stairs and a close-up of a face recoiling in shock. We did this to show something had happened, but the suspense came from the fact that you didn't know exactly what.* (Lisa)

> *We started filming from quite a close distance, and used a POV shot when Richard was angry, by filming over his shoulder to see my scared expression. We also chose to show how Richard had fallen by using a close-up of his foot tripping up. We also used a close-up to show that he had seriously been injured because there was blood on his head.* (Roger)

Designing games

In this Year 8 project, students explore the work of the games industry, and design and produce their own video game.

Learning about the games industry

The project was planned to introduce students to the media industries and institutions that lie behind the games they play. In many ways these are similar to other media industries, and often related to them through multinational corporations.

An introductory activity draws attention to the ways in which media industries are represented in the packaging of games. In order to compare the book, film and game of *Harry Potter and the Chamber of Secrets*, for example, the teacher and students collect all the logos of companies represented on the covers and boxes of these texts, which include:

- Warner Bros (which owns the name of *Harry Potter* and associated items as trademarks)
- Electronic Arts (which published the game)
- Knowwonder Digital Mediaworks (which developed the game)
- Bloomsbury (which published the book).

In addition, there are the logos of Ford (the texts include a flying Ford Anglia car), Microsoft, *Times Educational Supplement* (which had reviewed the book), Dolby sound (in the film), ELSPA (the European Leisure Software Publishers Association, which had rated the game as appropriate for children aged 3-plus).

The project simulates aspects of the way the games development industry works; so students are asked to propose names for a game studio, to write proposals for a game for students of their age, to work collaboratively in pairs and as a whole class to design and produce a multi-level game, and to design posters and write press releases and magazine reviews of the game on its completion.

Learning about the narrative systems of games

The game is planned as a whole-class activity. Students are asked, both in class discussion and for homework, to describe games they have played. Then the work moves on to planning a game. At this stage, central concepts of *narrative systems* in games are introduced. In many ways, these are similar to narratives in books and films, and can therefore consolidate and draw on students' prior knowledge of such systems. In other ways, they work differently. In particular, game narratives offer multiple routes, and are conditional: 'If you go down this corridor, you find the treasure; if you go down the other one, you meet the monster'. This conditionality, in the software used by the students for the project, is represented in a function called the 'rule-editor'.

All events in the game are constructed as a three-part sequence, represented in images and words, effectively as an if-clause: 'If the player | clicks on the sci-fi door | the sci-fi door opens'. This is a clear representation of the conditionality of game narratives, and the rules which govern them. Though there is no space here to develop the idea, this sequence is also representative of the language of computer programming; effectively, the students are programming a narrative. This provides the opportunity for cross-curricular collaboration between English, media and computing in schools, linking up understandings of narrative, representation and culture in one domain with programming, algorithms and databases in another.

Game narratives are also framed in a kind of permanent second-person address to the player, or its visual equivalent: you have these choices; you must open the box; you are the hero/heroine. This kind of work can produce more complex understandings of narrative and the grammatical structures which encode it.

Learning about ludic systems

The next stage is for students to learn about *ludic* or *game systems*. The software they will use to create their game is Missionmaker, a commercially produced authoring tool developed in a research project at the UCL Institute of Education. The teacher explains two aspects of game texts in introducing the students to Missionmaker. First, the idea of rule. Many accounts of games define them as rule-based systems (Juul, 2003; Salen and Zimmerman, 2003), and a brief consideration of other kinds of games (noughts and crosses, Monopoly, chess, football) shows that they are indeed based on clearly defined rules.

Students are encouraged to think of examples of rules across many kinds of game. One student, Joe, comes up with this list:

Call of Duty – you mustn't shoot your ally
Tennis – the ball mustn't leave the court
Pool – the white ball must not go down any of the pockets
Cards (pontoon) – you must not score more than 21 to win
Cricket – you can't touch the wickets with your bat.

Students are also asked to think about possible reasons for the importance of rules in games. Joe's explanation is:

The reason games have to have rules is because if there wasn't [sic] rules in a game you couldn't have challenges and boundries [sic], limits too, and that would spoil the fun and cause you not to have anything to complete. Rules are needed for objectives because they are almost the same thing because they are both telling you to do or not to do something.

This understanding recognises that rules make a game a different kind of text, as I will argue below: a text largely constructed in the imperative mood, which, rather than simply presenting you with a story, continuously demands that you act within that story.

The discussion also considers the paradox of why we enjoy following rules, which in contexts other than games and play can be oppressive. Joe continues the discussion with himself:

People enjoy following rules because it creates suspense of trying not to lose the game by breaking the rule, and a lot of people like difficult challenges. For example, on a computer game, trying not to be seen and to sneak somewhere where you are rewarded with a prize...

The other key concept within game systems is the idea of economies: quantifiable resources within games, such as health, hunger, power, currency, ammunition, food, healing potions. The teacher begins with the common-sense notion of economy as a monetary resource. In their written homework, students develop this idea for themselves, rooting it in their own knowledge of the world and experience of games. Felicity uses the example of *The Sims*:

Ideas of economy in a game (e.g. The Sims) is money as without it your 'sim' will not have a good life and you will find the gameplay much harder and less enjoyable as the sims get mad as they can't have many possessions and sometimes they don't have any food so they are really depressed.

Designing a class game

To begin planning the class game, students are asked to write individual proposals: short 'pitches' for a game, which have to include character sketches and examples of the rules and economies explored in class. Students' proposals are written for homework, and as many ideas as possible are synthesised by the teacher into a single plan. One girl suggests a game based on the melting of the polar icecaps due to global warming, as a result of which the protagonist loses his family and has to find and save them. Several others have thriller, assassin or secret-agent themes.

These ideas all become part of the eventual game: *Jimmie DeMora and the Dying World*, in which secret agent Jimmie DeMora has to find the evil corporation which is causing global flooding through its unscrupulous production of environmentally unfriendly fuels. Jimmie stops off for some shopping and saves members of his family along the way. A crucial part of the teacher's role here is mediating the students' proposals, partly by class discussion which opens up contradictions, differences, advantages and disadvantages, and partly by encouraging a consensus which will produce a coherent whole-class design to which, as far as possible, everyone in the class has contributed.

Clearly, this game has a central narrative. It also has game structures: levels, obstacles, rewards and clearly defined win-lose states. The player character is named Jimmie DeMora after a proposal by one of the class, who suggests a gangster-themed game with an assassin as central character (possibly influenced by games such as *Hitman 2: Silent Assassin*). However, as the class game design amalgamates elements from proposals by many of the students, the character is modified in terms of his mission and narrative background. He is equipped with a gun, but not to assassinate anyone: rather, to rescue members of his family, and to save the world, which is threatened by global warming and evil corporations.

Producing the game

The whole-game design is then divided up by the teacher into 15 levels, one for each pair of students in the class. This allows each pair to work on its own small game, with its own structure and sense of beginning and end. However, each pair has constantly to negotiate both with its adjacent pairs to see how the levels will connect with each other, and with other pairs to achieve other kinds of coherence; for instance, to make sure that NPCs (non-player characters) appearing in one level will look, behave and speak in the same way as the same characters appearing in another level later or earlier in the game.

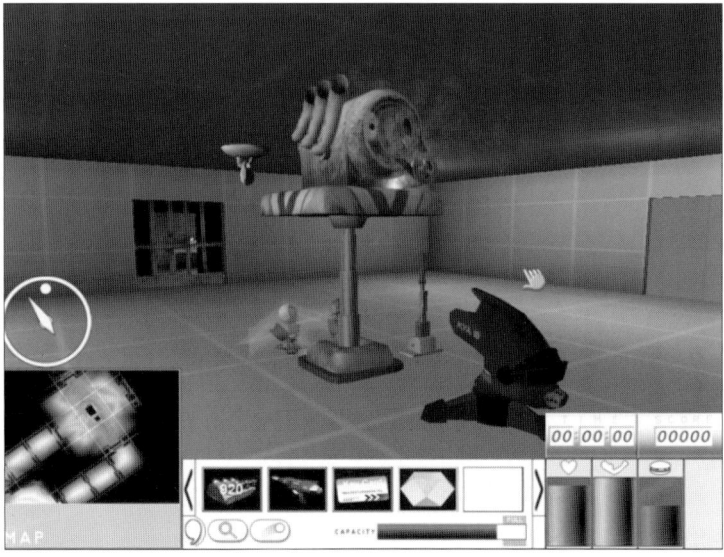

Figure 7: Screengrab from Jimmie DeMora and the Dying World

Figure 7 is a screen-grab from one of the levels of the game. It shows the point where the player, in first-person mode as Jimmie DeMora, has successfully overcome a series of obstacles and enemies to gain the source of green energy (the diamond visible in the player's inventory at the bottom of the screen), and to reach the generator powering the planet. The generator can only work if the player places the source of green energy into it.

This example shows that even designing one level of the whole-class game is a complex affair. These two students have made a satisfying narrative setting, appropriately 'dressed'; have designed characters to provide narrative opposition to the hero; and have created a sense of quest and of ending. At the same time, they have designed a coherent set of ludic elements: a mission, challenges, obstacles and rewards; rules; the related economies of ammunition and health; and a win-lose state.

'Publishing' the game

When the game of *Jimmie DeMora and the Dying World* is complete, the class is asked to think about the institutional context of game production again: to choose from activities such as making a poster to advertise the game, writing a review for the game magazine *Edge*, and writing a press release for the game's publication, including an imaginary interview with one of the game's designers. These activities further develop students' understanding of the work of media institutions, as well as the wider cultural context in which games are played, interpreted, enjoyed and critiqued.

Teaching *Psycho*

The sequence of this Year 9 project begins with a general exploration of the 'slasher' subgenre of films, using clips to show how Alfred Hitchcock's *Psycho* (1960) gave rise to a whole tradition which culminates in the ironic parodies of the *Scream* trilogy. The project then moves on to a viewing of *Psycho*, followed by whole-class analysis of specific clips, exploring how a multimodal analysis might look at dramatic movement and language, lighting, set design, props, shot framing and camera work, editing and music.

Next, the whole of the film is imported into the 'free' editing software Microsoft Moviemaker 2. This software has a function devised for people making their own videos: a function called 'clip detection', which splits up the incoming video into clips. What the software designers probably did not imagine was its function here: to anatomise the film into its hundreds of component shots.

The teacher is then able to ask many kinds of question, and to focus on aspects of the film language. If the students are asked to find examples of close-ups, reaction shots, long shots, cutaways and so on, they can find these at a glance. They can then move them to the timeline, instantly creating a new 'movie' made up of exemplars of a particular aspect of film grammar. They can also experiment with ways in which shots are combined, and explore questions of order, duration, sequence and other aspects of narrative.

In the next stage of the activity, students export clips and still images from Moviemaker into PowerPoint, to make a presentation about the meanings of *Psycho* and the formal languages that produce these meanings. The focus is on the characteristic affect of the horror film – fear.

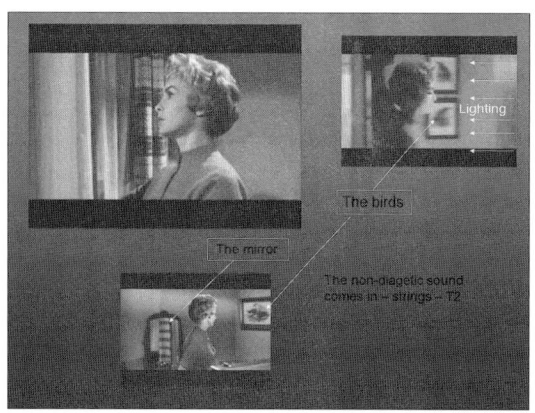
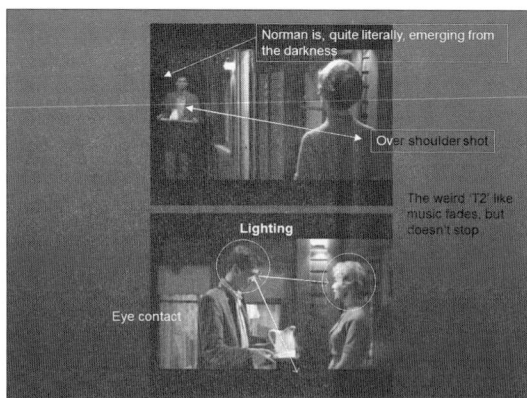

Figures 8, 9 and 10: Slides from Rosie's Psycho *presentation*

If we take one example, a presentation by Rosie (some slides from which are Figures 8, 9 and 10), we can see what kinds of meanings she analyses. She certainly explores traditional aspects of film language, such as *shot type* (she identifies close-ups and long shots), *camera movement* ('camera goes out with her'), and *non-diegetic sound* (sound other than that whose source is visible on the screen or is implied to be present by the action of the film; for example, mood music). However, she arguably pays more attention to dramatic aspects of the shots: 'Her body language is very nervous'; 'Looking around'; 'Closed-off body language'; 'Embarrassed, shy, sheepish'; 'Norman steps back'. She also looks closely at the significance of lighting: 'Face in shadow'; 'Norman is, quite literally, emerging from the darkness'. She comments on the significance of aspects of speech in a conversation between Norman and Marion, noting examples of hesitation, changing the subject, and one instance of Norman's identity dissolving into his mother's: 'Norman speaking for mother'.

Selling chocolate

This project was developed in collaboration with the UK charity organisation Comic Relief, much of whose work is channelled towards aid for Africa and support for sustainable development projects. In this case, Comic Relief wanted to link English schools with schools in Ghana to promote the idea of Fair Trade chocolate production. The chocolate was and is made by a London company, Divine Chocolate Ltd, 45% of which is owned by the Fair Trade cocoa-growers' co-operative Kuapa Kokoo in Ghana. The teacher in the school featured here suggested an additional element to the project: students would make a television advert for a new chocolate bar the company was launching: Dubble, marketed to children. Comic Relief agreed, and the school worked with Kika Dixon, the 'product champion' for Dubble at Divine, to develop a brief for a television advert. Kika visited the class of the students whose work is described below, and gave them the brief, just as she would to a professional advertising company. (A version of the project, including a video of Kika's project brief, is contained in the English and Media Centre's *Media Pack for GCSE* [Grahame, 2002].)

We could look more closely at this work in terms of the three categories offered in the rhetoric and poetics section of the previous chapter: *institutions*, *texts* and *audience*.

Institutions

In imagining that they were an advertising agency given a brief to produce an advert for a particular project, the students learned a great deal about the institutions involved in the production of fair-trade chocolate: Divine Chocolate itself; Divine's part-ownership by the Kuapa Kokoo co-operative, guaranteeing a fair price to the cocoa growers; other part-owners, including Body Shop International, Christian Aid and Comic Relief.

Texts

The students learned about three aspects of media texts: genre, representation and a number of features of the grammar of the moving image.

In terms of genre, the Dubble advert needed to be a hybrid. On the one hand, it should associate its product with a desirable lifestyle. On the other hand, it was inevitably a descendant of the 'charity ad' genre, once typified by sombre images of the victims of poverty, abuse and neglect, produced in the UK by charities such as Christian Aid, Oxfam and the National Society for the Prevention of Cruelty to Children, though it is fair to say that the first two of these organisations have worked since to produce more positive images of children in Africa.

This double lineage (to add to the many puns the name of the bar has intentionally spawned) led to a number of representational issues. Since Fair Trade intends to recognise the self-determination of African farmers, the typical charity-ad representation of passive victims needed to be avoided: no easy task given students' experience of these images of victimhood and aid. The representation of chocolate was an easier matter, at first glance; it simply needed to be shown in a positive light, and associated with desirable qualities, lifestyles or consequences. However, the chocolate itself had to be related to the Fair Trade theme, and this relationship was difficult to convey in an advertisement.

Audience

Students had to imagine an audience for their advert. The audience was specified in Kika Dixon's original brief: '11- to 16-year-olds, boys and girls'. How would the students' work represent the target group and their interests, aspirations, preoccupations? How would it construct a mode of address which would be comprehensible, engaging and credible? How would it locate the viewer?

One group of four boys constructed their advert as a narrative of chocolate-eating, associated with lifestyle qualities (the brief wanted messages like 'cool, cheeky, delicious'). The group found this narrative easy and enjoyable to imagine, plan and construct. The boys decided early on to recruit a friend from their year group as the star of the advert, and adopted an approach which several other groups also used: to show the boy buying the bar from the local corner shop, followed by some kind of transformation of his life.

The group found the Fair Trade message much harder to conceive and put across. The boys had real difficulty in imagining how the agency of African cocoa farmers might be represented. For them, as for other groups, part of this difficulty lay in a desire to represent Africa in a literal way. Eventually they asked if they could take their camera out of school to the Botanical Gardens in Cambridge and film lush tropical vegetation which they hoped could represent cocoa plantations.

Figure 11: Still from an advert for the Dubble chocolate bar

The result was a success. The music and its lyrics suggested a confident, urban teenage lifestyle, underlining the function of the boy as principal actor in the piece, the sequence cut to the rhythm of the music, suggesting his walk, his dance. The music and its rhythm were possibly stronger than any visual image in the first seconds of the ad, signalling the theme of the whole sequence as teenage identity, and subordinating the bar and the Fair Trade message to the rhythm throughout.

Filming performed poetry

This GCSE project aimed to integrate approaches from English and Media Studies projects. It evolved out of work by a Year 11 English group on the poem 'Search for My Tongue' by Sujata Bhatt.

The poem was part of an anthology of poetry to be studied for GCSE English (Assessment and Qualifications Alliance, no date). It evokes narratives of bilingualism, diaspora, the loss and rediscovery of mother tongue, and the way identity is not only expressed *in* language but is made of the stuff *of* language. It is also a poem about the body: specifically, about the organs of speech. It operates organic metaphors of plant life to signify the decay and regrowth of Gujarati in the mouth of the speaker: in her tongue, literally and figuratively.

The poem proved difficult for the class to engage with. It seemed remote from the experience of many of the students. So five bilingual students in the year group (speakers of Cantonese, Vietnamese, Bengali and French) were asked to write, perform and film poems modelled on Sujata Bhatt's. They were given a day off timetable to make short films of their poems, undertaking the filming and editing themselves.

These short films combined a variety of signifying modes – speech, facial expression, posture and gesture, the built environment, music – and filming and editing, the two orchestrating systems which bring together and organise all the modes that make up the moving image (Burn, 2013). In a small way, these films were dramatic texts, though the students wouldn't have thought of them in that way. The films dramatised something specific: the bilingual identities of the young poets. Identity across languages, cultures, countries and communities are the central metaphors of Sujata Bhatt's poem, and of the students' responses to it.

The central paradox in the filmed poems was the schism but also the unity of bilingualism; how it makes a whole person in whom the two languages are harmoniously united, but at the same time is a symbol and an effect of cultural difference.

Fatima says:

> *My life is split into two pieces*
> *Like a fruit that has been cut into two halves.*

For her, the difference between Bengali and English is a marked thing: the voices jostle for control, like disobedient children, emphasising the split between worlds and cultures which bilingualism entails. Fatima is also cannily aware of the confusion and difficulty of language, how it can trip you up as well as bravely represent your dual identity:

> *Voices can make a fool out of you.*

She chooses to perform against a stark brick wall, whose uncompromising materiality carries messages of its own. She decides to film from two different angles, so that she is shown in three-quarter profile, from one side for the English parts, from the other for the Bengali (Figures 12 and 13). This strong device is a visual transformation of the first lines of her poem, but says something different from the fruit simile – something more like 'I am a speaker who faces in two directions'. The distinction between the languages is sharply marked by the transition between the alternating shots, which is always a cut.

Figures 12 and 13: The alternating angles used by Fatima to represent English and Bengali speech

Fatima also chooses different framings, which change the meaning of the lines. A command to one of her two voices to be quiet is a good example. The English version – 'Quiet!' – shows a head-and-shoulders close-up, facing left; the Bengali version – 'Chup thako!' – is an extreme close-up of her mouth (Figure 14). This second shot associates the spoken Bengali more emphatically with the organ of speech, representing this language more intimately.

The project is a good example of the balance between rhetoric and poetics, and of how such a balance can be explored across literary and media texts. The integration of the two forms, poetry and film, works to represent the rhetorical message of the texts about the value of bilingualism, employing the aesthetic devices of verse and the moving image to do so.

Figure 14: Close-up of Fatima's mouth, emphasising the Bengali reprimand

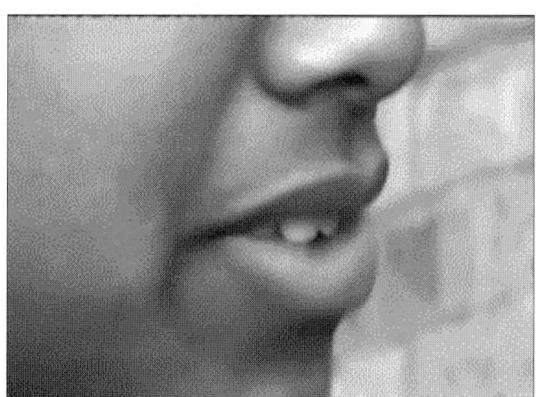

6 An outline framework for a media-education curriculum

Introduction

Furthermore, in both drama and media study, insufficient attention is given to progression, with students doing similar activities and demonstrating similar skills from year to year, such as 'freeze-frames' and 'hot-seating' in drama, and simple storyboards or advertisements in media work. It remains rare for secondary schools, either individually or working with their primary feeder schools, to consider in any detail how students' media literacy is developed through the English or wider curriculum. (Office for Standards in Education, *English in Secondary Schools*, 2004)

This judgement by England's education watchdog is a fair reflection of the fragmentary nature of media education in this country, and of the consequential lack of any real sense of progression. Until now, the substantial tradition of media work in the UK has mainly been in the public-examination courses in Media Studies, which have been the engines of curricular development, the providers of much of the in-service training, and the innovators in production technologies.

Institutions which specialise in media education in the UK have made their own suggestions for a media-education curriculum. The British Film Institute has proposed a model in stages that roughly correspond to the Key Stages of the National Curriculum, though the authors are careful to emphasise that their stages are not necessarily age-specific (Film Education Working Group, 1999). While this model has been a valuable contribution to the debate about progression, it is limited by its focus on 'cine-literacy', and by its assumption that specific knowledge and concepts can be assigned to specific stages of development. So, for example, students at Stage 1 would learn about 'long shot' and 'close-up', and those at Stage 2 would learn about 'angle' and 'frame'.

While students' conceptual understandings of the media do become more sophisticated as they get older, it is hard to see how this kind of staged progression would work. However, the BFI has also initiated teacher action-research projects looking at progression, as part of the Best Practice Research Scholarships funded by the government in the 1990s. Meanwhile, my involvement in a project exploring learning progression in media education across primary and secondary schools has informed the framework which follows.

Perhaps the most detailed picture of how progression in the secondary years might take place appears in the English and Media Centre's resource packs: *The Media Book*, which provides resources and guidance linked to the National Curriculum for 11 to 14 (Grahame and Domaille, 2001); and the *Media Pack for GCSE* (Grahame, 2002), which contains five units of work for GCSE English Language or Media Studies.

As with language and literacy in general, the best model for progression in media education is recursive. It is impossible to say that we will artificially withhold knowledge of how to edit sequences of film, or how to frame a shot, or how to write a script, in our work with seven-year-olds. In a general sense, a film-production project with young children is the same as such a project with 16-year-olds, and might involve the full array of signifying practices. The shape of progression is the repetition of such work over and over again, just as work in English always involves, for example, reading literature and producing factual and imaginative writing.

Whatever it is that changes as learners move through the years is better understood as expansion than as addition: expansion of concepts, of metalanguage, of media forms, of cultural purposes and cultural horizons. The following proposals for a media-education curriculum are based on these assumptions.

The framework's structure

Within each age group, the proposals fall into three categories: reading media, writing media and setting the media in their context. As with other booklets in this series, the age groups are broad. There is no attempt to sub-divide Key Stages 1 and 2, as happens in the programmes of study for reading and writing in the new National Curriculum for English; and there are combined proposals for Key Stages 3 and 4. Teachers are in the best position to know when learners within these broad age groups are capable of taking on new challenges, both as receivers and interpreters and as producers of media.

Early Years Foundation Stage

Reading Media	• Children view children's TV programmes and films together in class. They talk about these experiences, expressing their own likes and dislikes.
Writing Media	• Children role-play favourite characters from TV and film.
	• They re-present their favourite films, programmes and other media (for example, by making posters of them).
Setting the media in their context	• Children discuss friends' and family's media preferences.
	• They discuss rules about media use in the family and school; they invent their own rules.

Key Stage 1

Reading media	• Pupils collectively experience, enjoy and discuss different media, especially film, TV and games.
	• They explore early understandings of who makes the media.
	• They explore early understandings of how media texts are put together to make meaning.
	• They explore early understandings of media audiences, moving from themselves and their families to others.
Writing media	• Pupils make short print-media texts, including comics and magazines.
	• They make, act for and edit short films.
Setting the media in their context	• Pupils explore how texts are connected (for example, how the *Harry Potter* stories exist as books, films, games and merchandise).
	• They explore media histories (for example, how adverts from the 1950s are different from today's).
	• They explore media regulation further (for example, by being taught about and discussing the TV watershed).

Key Stage 2

Reading media	• Pupils collectively experience, enjoy and discuss a wider range of media: for example, TV and film (including full-length movies), some printed media, advertising and games.
	• They organise media texts in categories such as genre.
	• They compare their own media preferences with those of others.
	• They explore media institutions and audiences through practical research projects.
Writing media	• Pupils make more complex media texts, such as news broadcasts, longer edited films, simple video games, and websites/blogs. They re-present their own experiences of film, TV, print media, games and social media in these productions.
	• They make media texts to represent ideas, social groups and individuals.
	• They make media texts for identified audiences.
Setting the media in their context	• Pupils explore more complex links between texts, such as remakes and adaptations over time.
	• They explore links between texts and narratives in English, drama and media (for example, book, stage adaptation, film and video games of Pullman's *Northern Lights*).
	• They explore more detailed regulatory practices, such as age-labelling systems on films and games, and discuss who produces them.

Key Stages 3 and 4

Reading media	• Students continue collectively to experience, enjoy and discuss moving-image texts of many kinds (for example cinema films, factual and dramatic TV programmes, YouTube clips, computer games), texts from the printed media, and texts which combine different modes (for example, websites carrying writing, images and sound).
	• They consider complex meanings such as ambiguity, through close analysis of media texts.
	• They research media institutions (broadcasters, news conglomerates, game companies) and their practices, motivations and functions.
	• They consider complex audience formations in relation to social class, gender and ethnicity; and how audiences are becoming producers in the digital age.
Writing media	• Students continue to make media texts in different forms, developing more complex skills for example in filming, visual design of printed media, editing, game design and online media design (for example, navigation, hyperlinking, uses of widgets and plug-ins).
	• They continue to develop complex representations of themselves, of their peers, of other individuals and groups in society, and of ideas.
	• They simulate media institutions (for example, film and television production companies, museums and cinemas, newspapers, film agencies and institutes, regulators, broadcasters, game developers, social media start-ups, archives) in their own productions.
	• They develop further their understandings of media audiences: across social groups, over time, internationally, across and between different media.
Setting the media in their context	• Students continue to explore, through research, simulation and creative practice, the wider contexts of media culture: taste, pleasure and cultural value; the functions of the media in entertainment, high art, popular culture, politics and education; the relationship between the media arts and the digital sciences (for example, in computer-generated imaging in films, electronic design of newspapers and magazines, the programming of games).

7 Conclusion: beyond the old divides

English and media education belong together. They need and support each other; they stimulate and enliven each other; they also serve as correctives to each other's prejudices, restrictions of scope and intellectual limitations. The theoretical models, the history and the examples offered in this booklet are intended to move beyond the sterile polarities constructed by mandatory curricula in the UK, beyond the opposed stances of suspicion and reverence applied respectively to media texts and literary texts.

Literature is out of its jacket, marked with the signs of its economic and material production, bleeding into other media, subject to the online transformations of fans able to rewrite the hallowed word with no respect for textual boundaries. Conversely, films, television drama, comic books and computer games have grown their own respectable histories, canons and heroic author-figures. They are collected, revered, curated, acknowledged by the institutions of high art which once reserved their attention for the traditional elite arts.

In this world of cultural reversals, English and media teachers owe it to their students to make common cause: to embrace models of literacy which collapse the boundaries between elite and popular culture, between today's and yesterday's cultural moment, between the meaning and the structure of texts, between texts' use of language and of other modes. Nothing will be lost, and there is much to gain.

References

Assessment and Qualifications Alliance (no date) *AQA Anthology*. Manchester: Assessment and Qualifications Alliance.

Banaji, S. and Burn, A. with Buckingham, D. (2007) *The Rhetorics of Creativity: a Literature Review*. London: Creative Partnerships. Available at: http://www.creativitycultureeducation.org/the-rhetorics-of-creativity-a-literature-review Accessed 26 March 2015.

Bazalgette, C. (2008) The Development of Media Education in England: A Personal View, in J. Flood, S. Heath and D. Lapp (eds.) *Handbook of research on teaching literacy through the communicative and visual arts. Volume II*. New York: Lawrence Erlbaum.

Bearne, E. and Bazalgette, C. (2010) *Beyond Words: Developing Children's Understanding of Multimodal Texts*. Leicester: United Kingdom Literacy Association.

Buckingham, D. (1998) *Teaching Popular Culture: Beyond Radical Pedagogy (Media, Education and Culture)*. London: Routledge.

Buckingham, D. (2003) *Media Education: Literacy, learning and contemporary culture*. Oxford: Polity.

Buckingham, D. and Sefton-Green, J. (1994) *Cultural Studies Goes to School: Reading and Teaching Popular Media*. London: Taylor and Francis.

Buckingham, D. and Bazalgette, C. (eds.) (1995) *In Front of the Children: Screen Entertainment and Young Audiences*. London: British Film Institute.

Burn, A. (2013) The Kineikonic Mode: Towards a Multimodal Approach to Moving Image Media, in C. Jewitt (ed.) *The Routledge Handbook of Multimodal Analysis*. London: Routledge.

Burn, A. and Durran, J. (2007) *Media Literacy in Schools: Practice, Production, Progression*. London: Paul Chapman.

Burn, A. and Parker, D. (2003) *Analysing Media Texts*. London: Continuum.

Connor, S. (1992) *Theory and Cultural Value*. Oxford: Blackwell.

The Cox Committee (1989) *English for ages 5-16* (The Cox Report). London: Her Majesty's Stationery Office. Available at: http://www.educationengland.org.uk/documents/cox1989/cox89.html Accessed 9 March 2015.

Department for Culture, Media and Sport (2012) *Cultural Education in England* (The Henley Review). London: Her Majesty's Stationery Office. Available at: https://www.gov.uk/government/uploads/system/uploads/attachment_data/file/260726/Cultural_Education_report.pdf Accessed 26 March 2015.

Department for Education (2014) *The national curriculum in England: Framework document*. London: Department for Education. Available at: https://www.gov.uk/government/uploads/system/uploads/attachment_data/file/381344/Master_final_national_curriculum_28_Nov.pdf Accessed 23 March 2015.

Film Education Working Group (1999) *Making Movies Matter*. London: British Film Institute. Available at: http://sic.conaculta.gob.mx/centrodoc_documentos/21.pdf Accessed 23 March 2015.

Genette, G. (1980) *Narrative Discourse*. Oxford: Blackwell.

Grahame, J. (2002) *Media Pack for GCSE*. London: English and Media Centre. Telephone: 0207 359 8080.

Grahame, J. and Domaille, K. (2001) *The Media Book*. London: English and Media Centre. Available at: http://www.englishandmedia.co.uk/publications/cat_detail.php?itemID=17&title=THE%20MEDIA%20BOOK Accessed 9 March 2015.

Hall, S. and Whannell, P. (1965) *The Popular Arts*. New York: Pantheon Books.

Huizinga, J. (1949) *Homo Ludens: a Study of the Play Element in Culture*. London: Routledge and Kegan Paul.

Jenkins, H. (2006) *Convergence Culture: Where Old and New Media Collide*. New York: New York University Press.

Jewitt, C. and Kress, G. (eds.) (2003) *Multimodal Literacy*. New York: Peter Lang.

Juul, J. (2003) The Game, the Player, the World: Looking for a Heart of Gameness, in *Level Up: Digital Games Research Conference Proceedings*, M. Copier and J. Raessens (eds.). Utrecht: Utrecht University, pp. 30-45. Available at: http://www.jesperjuul.net/text/gameplayerworld/ Accessed 23 March 2015.

Kelland, M., Morris, D. and Lloyd, D. (2005) *Machinima*. Boston, MA: Thomson.

Kress, G. and van Leeuwen, T. (1996) *Reading Images: the Grammar of Visual Design*. London: Routledge

Kress, G. and van Leeuwen, T. (2000) *Multimodal Discourse: The Modes and Media of Contemporary Communication*. London: Hodder Arnold.

Leavis, F.R. (1948) *The Great Tradition: George Eliot, Henry James, Joseph Conrad*. London: Chatto and Windus.

Leavis, F.R. and Thompson, D. (1933/1977) *Culture and Environment: The Training of Critical Awareness*. Westport, CT: Greenwood Press.

Lord, A. (1960) *The Singer of Tales*. Cambridge, MA: Harvard University Press.

Manovich, L. (1998) *The Language of New Media*. Cambridge, MA: MIT Press.

Marsh, J. and Larson, J. (2005) *Making Literacy Real: Theories and Practices for Learning and Teaching*. London: Sage.

Masterman, L. (1980) *Teaching About Television*. London: MacMillan.

McDougall, J. (2006) *The Media Teacher's Book*. London: Hodder Education.

Northern Ireland Screen (2004) *A Wider Literacy*. Belfast: Northern Ireland Screen. Available at: http://www.northernirelandscreen.co.uk/DatabaseDocs/doc_80243.pdf Accessed 23 March 2015.

Office for Standards in Education (2004) *English in Secondary Schools*. London: Office for Standards in Education.

Ong, W. (1982) *Orality and Literacy: the Technologizing of the Word*. London: Methuen.

Parry, M. (1930) Studies in the Epic Technique of Oral Verse-Making. I: Homer and Homeric Style, in *Harvard Studies in Classical Philology Vol. 41*. Cambridge, MA: Harvard University Press, pp. 73-143.

Potter, J. (2005) 'This Brings Back a Lot of Memories' – a case study in the analysis of digital video production by young learners, in *Education, Communication and Information, Vol. 5, No 1*. London: Taylor and Francis Online, pp. 5-23. Available at: http://www.tandfonline.com/toc/reci20/current#.VQ_97XZTtvA Accessed 23 March 2015.

Qualifications and Curriculum Authority (2005) *English 21/playback: a national conversation on the future of English*. London: Her Majesty's Stationery Office.

Qualifications and Curriculum Authority (2007) *The National Curriculum for England and Wales*. London: Her Majesty's Stationery Office.

Reid, M., Burn, A. and Parker, D. (2002) *Evaluation Report of the BECTA Digital Video Pilot Project*. Coventry: BECTA. Available at: http://homepages.shu.ac.uk/~edsjlc/ict/becta/research_papers/what_the_research_says/dvreport_241002.pdf Accessed 26 March 2015.